In memory of two King's Cross campaigners,

Phil Jeffries and Lisa Pontecorvo

King's Cross:
A Sense of Place

Angela Inglis with Nigel Buckner

Front cover photo: 34 - 40 York Way, 2010

Back cover photo: Battlebridge Basin, 2009

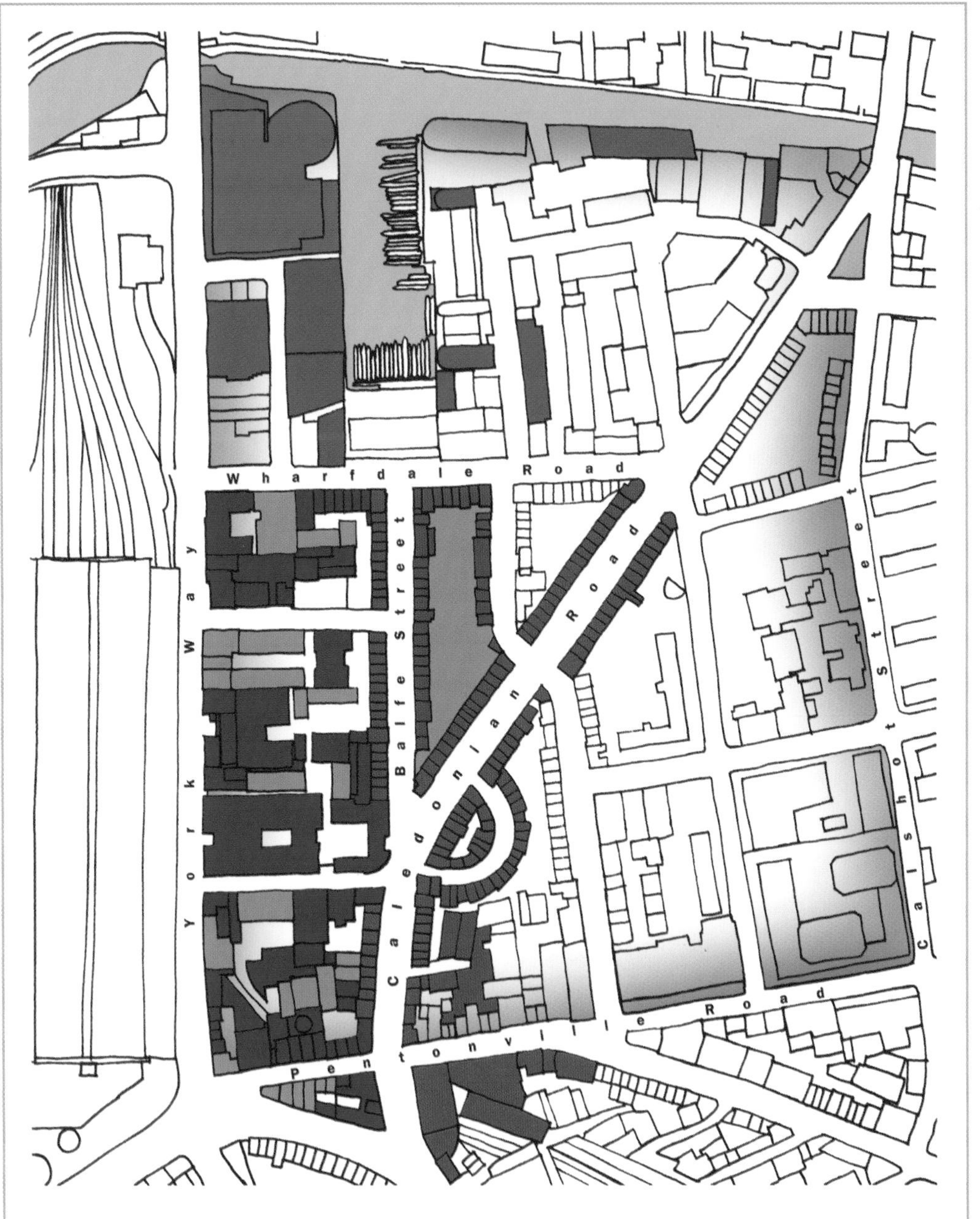

Areas covered in the book, coloured to indicate relevant chapters

Map: A. Delarue

Contents

Foreword

by Lord Chris Smith

This is the story of a remarkable, unique corner of London. It traces some of the history. It explores the challenges that have faced King's Cross through recent years – and poor old King's Cross has had a lot thrown at it during this period. Above all, it tells the story of a community that fought back: against insensitive developers; against disruption, decay, and destruction; and against anyone who saw King's Cross only as a place to pass through rather than as a place to live in and to savour. The community spirit, and some of the heroic people who fostered and led it, fill the pages of this book. It's an inspiring story, and its result has been a real transformation of a place, for the better. It's a story worth telling, and worth reading.

Introduction

by Angela Inglis

The book started with the idea of a photographic record of how the plan to build an international railway station at King's Cross was thrown out in favour of St Pancras. I had recently published 'Railway Lands', a photographic book about the changing landscape around St Pancras before and during the building of the international station there. It occurred to me that the local people's campaigns against the previous proposal at King's Cross was something to be investigated further and the story told.

As I began my research and met some of the prime movers in this fiercely fought battle, I became aware of two other adjacent areas where campaigns were successfully fought one after the other. Balfe Street and the lower part of Caledonian Road ('South Cally') featured in all three. My research expanded, leading me to key people who had been involved. Thus the book has become a truly collaborative effort, with contributions from a wide range of people including many involved at first hand.

The first three chapters, forming Part One, tell three stories. Chapter 1 is Norma Steel's, of how she and her family saved her home in Balfe Street from the bulldozers. Chapter 2 is Randal Keynes' account of the successful local campaign to fight the King's Cross Railway Bill in order to save homes and businesses, focusing on the South Cally area where he lived. Chapter 3 tells how local people constructively argued to save a precious industrial legacy and get a mixed use development in the area now known as the Regent Quarter, extending west to York Way.

All three stories show determination with clear goals. Each campaign enlisted residents, councillors, architects, planners and lawyers to assist them. In the Regent Quarter campaign recounted in Chapter 3 the case was put so well that the developer, P&O, under the leadership of Gary Brooks, bit the bullet and set about talking to local people, asking them what they really wanted. Through realistic discussion and compromise a solution was found, surely a model for future generations.

Part Two takes the longer, more leisurely view, looking at the historical and 'concrete' aspects of the area, in contrast to the human focus of Part One. In Chapter 4, Malcolm Tucker, engineering historian and industrial archaeologist, looks at the sites of past industry in what once was called Battle Bridge, and in Chapter 5 he presents the story of Battlebridge Basin on the canal. As with many old names spelling can vary.

Chapter 6 completes the book. Photographs illustrate Peter Millican's Kings Place which stands directly north and very close to the campaign areas featured in Part One. It is described by its architect, Sir Jeremy Dixon, while Alec Forshaw, then Islington Conservation Officer, writes about his involvement in its genesis. Completed in October 2008 it has established itself as a thriving centre for music, the arts and business.

From its beginnings as a photographic record, this book has instead turned out to be a collaborative history told as much through the narrative as through the photographs. King's Cross is an area full of stories waiting to be told, and inevitably one book cannot do justice to them all.

I should like to thank all the people who have contributed generously to this project in interviews, in writing or with photographs and maps. Additional thanks go to Malcolm Tucker for his fascinating historical perspective and his help with technical detail in many parts of the book, to Mike Bruce, Alec Forshaw, Barbara Jacobson, Randal Keynes, Martin Lipson, Paul Lowenberg and Lester Pritchard for their contributions to Part One. I should particularly like to thank Jeannie Burnett, Diana Shelley and Norma Steel for their support throughout this project and for introducing me to many of the key players, to Peter Millican for his interest and encouragement and to Tim Burnett for his editing skills. Full acknowledgements can be found on page 226.

Finally, I am indebted to Nigel Buckner, for his design expertise, and for travelling with me so patiently on this King's Cross journey.

Battle Bridge

Artist: Unknown, from a sketch book of 1812. Probably taken from the north of the hamlet.
Courtesy: Randal Keynes

Part One:

The battle for Balfe Street

Railway threat, blight and survival

Regent Quarter

Norma, around 1950, with neighbour's little girl, Sue Palmer, in Balfe Street.
Photo: Supplied by Norma Steel

Chapter 1

The battle for Balfe Street

The story of Norma Steel

by Angela Inglis

Introduction

Norma Steel is an archetypal King's Cross campaigner. In the 1980s and 90s she was one of many who fought successfully against the international station then proposed for King's Cross, and the demolition which that would have entailed.

But by then Norma had been blooded in the battle for Balfe Street. In the 1970s and 80s she campaigned with others in 'The Cross' to save homes on Balfe Street from the bulldozer. The reason they stand there today is because of hard and successful campaigning in which Norma and her family took part.

In most community campaigns natural leaders emerge. Norma was one of them. Her affection for her family and community sustained her till the battle for Balfe Street was won. Those who campaigned with her pay generous tribute to the role she played.

Balfe Street campaigners also benefited from some important initiatives from Islington Council. In reality it was a two pronged attack.

I am grateful to those mentioned in this chapter who brought special skills and expertise in piloting the campaign. But through Norma's eyes one glimpses the raw energy, the fun and shared enjoyment which fuelled this dynamic campaign.

Top left: Norma Steel, July 2010, in the garden that she and her neighbours created with the help of Islington Council in the mid 1980s. *Photo: Angela Inglis*

Bottom left: Battlebridge Garden, 1995 with Sally (left), Norma's daughter, Norma Steel and Norma's mother Clara, in front of the piano. *Photo: Supplied by Norma Steel*

Right: Norma Steel's husband Frank Steel (right), with a friend in Balfe Street. *Photo: Supplied by Norma Steel*

The battle for Balfe Street

Clara Brown, Norma Steel's mother, was born in 1905 and moved to 23 Albion Street (now Balfe Street) off the south end of Caledonian Road when she was six months old. Clara remained in the family home when she married George Brown.[1]

Norma, born in 1938, was raised in the same house and when she married Frank Steel in 1956, they lived on the upper floor while her mother and father lived on the lower floor. Norma's daughter, Sally, born in 1963, was also raised in Balfe Street.[2]

Norma and her family were a vital part of their neighbourhood. Clara, her mother, entertained people by playing piano in the Star and Garter and many other local pubs. Hence Norma was known as the 'star baby'.[3] In her King's Cross Voices interview Clara says,[4] 'my grandma taught Madame Tussaud how to play piano. But we never used music – it was all by ear, we played very old songs, *Abba Dabba, The Very Thought of You, Who's Sorry Now, Swanee, Red Red Robin, Rock-a-bye Your Baby*. I played for the silent films, cowboy and Indian films, at the Cosy Corner Electric Cinema in Pentonville Road. My husband used to sing Al Jolson songs and asked me to play piano for him. That's how I met him.' An Evening Standard Interview by Paul Barker in 1989 states:[5] Mrs Brown remembers the vast Scala Cinema which had been built at King's Cross in the 1920s. 'It was lovely inside with a wonderful organ.'

In a King's Cross Interview[6] Norma recalls a very happy childhood despite the second world war. 'There were so many children in Balfe Street. It was just one long fun period in spite of warnings, blackouts or shrapnel coming out of the sky.'

Norma values the freedom she enjoyed as a young girl. At the age of ten she would take the neighbour's baby, Sue Palmer, right across London to visit Norma's cousins. 'It seemed such a normal thing to do.'[7]

Balfe Street Area

The Balfe Street neighbourhood remember Norma vividly. Returning to Balfe Street in 2011 from her current home in Barnet she encountered Andrew Pacheco, an old Spanish friend[8] (see photo on next page). He disappeared into his house and returned with a huge bottle of Taittinger champagne to celebrate their reunion after ten years.

Balfe Street is an area of King's Cross that had been threatened with demolition both before and after World War II. In 1973 Norma suspected that they were in danger of losing their home[9] when the owners, York Way Motors, stopped collecting the rent. Norma's cousin, a quantity surveyor, sent her an article from which she deduced that the property developer, D and J Levy, under the name of Stock Conversion, had acquired property in Balfe Street without informing the tenants. They gave the name Saffron Properties to that part of their company then responsible for Balfe Street. Once Norma and her family knew this they insisted on paying their rent. This reduced the likelihood of them being evicted. As tenants moved out of the houses and properties became vacant, Stock Conversion would board them up, and cease doing repairs. They wanted to demolish the west side of Balfe Street as part of a multi-million square foot office development.[10]

At this stage Martin Lipson was employed by Islington Council for Community Relations to set up the THornhill Neighbourhood Project whose aim was to support people in on of London's most deprived communities, and to help to help improve living conditions. In April 1973 Martin started making contact with local residents, hoping to find out what was happening in 'The Cross' with regard to development. Martin had set up a neighbourhood advice centre in Copenhagen Street, funded by Islington Council, to help local groups in the area. One of the first people he met was Norma, who introduced him to others in 'The Cross'.[11] Norma says 'this meeting was manna from heaven'.[12]

It soon became apparent that the threats to the community needed an organised response, and Martin encouraged them to form the King's Cross Community Association. In helping the new group to fight a proposed development in the Battlebridge Basin Martin Lipson and Anthony Rossi wrote a key paper,[13] which was delivered at the Battlebridge Local Inquiry in 1974. It first defined the area by saying[14] that 'most of the King's Cross

Map: A. Delarue

Top: Norma encountering Andrew Pacheco, an old friend, outside his house in Balfe Street, 2011. *Photo: Angela Inglis*
Bottom: Martin Lipson in 2011. As lead worker of the Thornhill Neighbourhood Project, Martin encouraged the formation of the King's Cross Community Association. *Photo: Angela Inglis*

community, 1350 people, are living in five streets; Caledonian Road, Northdown Street, Balfe Street, Wharfdale Road and Keystone Crescent being bounded by the Regent's Canal to the north and Pentonville Road to the south, York Way to the west and Calshot Street to the east... The community is physically isolated from its surroundings by busy roads, the blank walls of King's Cross Station and goods yard, and the Regent's Canal... there are a disturbingly large number of decaying empty houses, vacant sites and redundant factories and warehouses... no open space whatsoever within or close to the neighbourhood, and the only adventure playground has been closed down indefinitely...'

'The Association by building up community involvement in the possibilities of a better King's Cross for its residents is desperately trying to avoid the frightening precedents of similar communities having been destroyed by inaction and indifferent development. Tolmer Square and the Euston Tower are close by and in identical locations relative to the inner core of London, and they show all too well what can happen to 'The Cross'.[15]

The Community's concern, according to this paper, was that the people living in the King's Cross area should remain where they were. Lipson and Rossi devised a five point plan:[16]

'1. Local people who choose to stay should have priority for re-housing in local improved houses (e.g. on the Caledonian Road) and their vacated homes should be improved for other local people to move into.

2. The Council should give discretionary grants for existing occupiers or tenants to improve their homes.

3. Existing empty houses should be taken over by the Council or a housing association for improvement and the housing of local people.

4. No permissions for office developments in the area should be granted until an overall plan had been agreed.

Top left: Lester Prichard headed a planning team to deal with blighted areas in the borough of Islington. *Photo: Angela Inglis*
Top right: Gordon Arnot was a key campaigner and tireless in his work. *Photo: Supplied by Norma Steel*
Bottom: Margaret Hodge, who was then in Islington Council (see opposite). Her tireless efforts greatly facilitated conservation in King's Cross. *Photo: Angela Inglis*

5. Islington Council and the GLC must make firm commitments about the future of King's Cross, with the strongest possible emphasis on the needs and wishes of the existing community.'

Just after Norma and her family had secured their tenancy with Saffron Properties Norma began work in earnest to secure the future of the Balfe Street and neighbouring community. They were helped by Margaret Hodge, Chair of Islington's Housing Committee, 1973 – 1981, and Leader of Islington Council from 1982 to 1992.[17]

Margaret Hodge was aided from January 1974 onwards by a special team in the Planning Department led by Lester Pritchard[18] to deal with the blighted areas of the borough. The top priorities were the Angel and King's Cross. The area between York Way and Caledonian Road had been zoned by the GLC (and previously the LCC for many years) for industrial development. In the early 1970s the GLC declared most of the houses in Balfe and Northdown Streets as a slum clearance area. Islington negotiated with the GLC to stop this clearance, and in 1975 the GLC offered to sell all the houses and land they owned in the area to Islington.

Another person who brought significant expertise to the campaign was Paul Lowenberg.[19] In 1974 he had come to the London School of Economics to do post graduate research on urban development. The following spring there was a notice placed seeking volunteers to help with the development of the King's Cross Community Association. Paul went to a meeting of the group where he met Norma and started his long involvement with them. He and a friend were helped by Norma to climb over her wall into the house next door, 25 Balfe Street (a house that had been left empty and derelict for several years by the owners, Stock Conversion), where they became squatters, thus protecting that house from further deterioration and possible demolition. Paul was conversant with planning procedures and acted as a link between the neighbourhood project and Islington Council. He worked closely with Norma and others in the community. They have remained friends and she still sings his praises for his expertise and commitment to the area.

Top left: Paul Lowenberg squatted the house next to Norma's and brought expertise to the campaigns. *Photo: Angela Inglis*
Top right: Barbara Jacobson. She also squatted the house next to Norma's and became involved in the campaign. *Photo: Angela Inglis*
Bottom: Residents campaign for a communal garden. Left of the banner in the foreground is Norma and her daughter.
Photo: R.M. Stevenson.

In 1975 Paul Lowenberg helped the community to make representations[20] to get the houses on the west side of Balfe Street, 5-35, listed. The window and brick details on these houses were excellent examples of mid-nineteenth century housing design with the sash windows framed by semi-circular-relieving arches, a nineteenth century Islington feature, although found elsewhere in London. They were successful.

According to Lester Pritchard's records,[21] 'in January 1976, Islington accepted the GLC's offer to sell them the houses and land they owned in the slum clearance area and nearly all the houses were agreed for rehabilitation. In 1977 the whole of the area was included in the Keystone Crescent Conservation Area. This meant that the buildings could not be demolished without the express consent of the Council, or the Government on appeal. This extended the protection which had been granted to 5-35 Balfe Street when they were listed in 1975. Following the purchase of the GLC houses and land, the Council then made a Compulsory Purchase Order on the Stock Conversion houses in Balfe Street, with a provision for the gardens to be extended in due course.'

In 1976 Martin Lipson left the Thornhill Neighbourhood Project to work in neighbouring Haringey and was replaced by Gordon Arnot who remained until 1998. According to Norma he was a key campaigner and tireless in his work.[22]

Paul Lowenberg joined the Thornhill Neighbourhood Project as a full-time worker in 1977 and worked there for three years.[23] During this period, not only did the King's Cross Community Association, with assistance from the Thornhill Neighbourhood Project, get the Council to agree a strategy to preserve the houses, and compulsarily purchase property where the landlords refused to make improvements, but they also led successful opposition to major road plans and were able to get the NHS to agree to improve provision of GP services in the area, which ultimately led to the construction of a new primary health care facility on Killick Street. (See Appendix 1 immediately after this chapter.) Paul was also appointed as a Director of the King's Cross Property Company, set up by the Greater London Development Agency, to take responsibility for commercial property owned by the GLC, particularly around Battlebridge Basin. Through this

Top: Reconstruction takes place in Northdown Street.
Photo: Supplied by Norma Steel
Bottom: Northdown Street in June 2010. *Photo: Angela Inglis*

company key buildings were saved from demolition and eventually renewal schemes proceeded, including the East side of Crinan Street and the west side of Wharf Road.

Examining the facts, it seems clear that this successful saving of an area was a two pronged effort, from the campaigners and from Islington Council. The Thornhill Neighbourhood Project News Sheet in March, 1976, announced[24] 'Islington Council's Housing Committee have suddenly decided to pull down one side of Balfe Street. The King's Cross Community Association are very angry about this. Despite the joint Housing Sub-Committee with the Council, on which local residents sit, they were not consulted beforehand. Now the Community Association is sending a deputation to the next full Council meeting in the hope of deferring this decision until later'.

Little did the Community Association know at that point about Islington's decision to buy the houses and land, but one can imagine the delight when they were told the good news, and in addition when they were told about the Conservation Area and the fact that the houses were to be rehabilitated.

Norma confirms the help that she received from Islington Council:[25] 'in the seventies and early eighties Margaret Hodge oversaw the buying of houses in Balfe and Northdown Streets many of which had to be completely rebuilt'. Norma and fellow residents working for the Thornhill Neighbourhood Project benefited enormously from this policy. She says: 'Margaret Hodge worked very hard, I have lots of respect for her. She would meet anytime, even in lunch hours and the houses did get rehabilitated. Islington Council were involved all the way along. It was a lot of work, meetings. All voluntary. The planning committee meeting would sometimes go on until 1 a.m.' Norma also acknowledges the work that Lester Pritchard did in conserving the area.[26]

In 1978 Norma's family moved into refurbished houses: Clara, her mother, to 34 Balfe Street, her aunt to 35, her mother-in-law into 40A, and her sister-in-law into 40B. Norma, her husband, Frank, and her daughter, Sally, moved to 73 Northdown Street in early 1979 and eventually bought that house. Norma says that, for sentimental reasons, her family brought the metal bath tub from 23 Balfe Street and put it in the garden of their

Left: Balfe Street from Caledonian Road, April 2010.
Photo: Angela Inglis

Right: Norma's family paid for cherry trees to be planted. Today the trees remain and every spring the street is full of blossom. Norma's mother, Clara Brown, cried when she saw the trees. *Photo: Angela Inglis*

Northdown Street house. Before Norma's family left Balfe Street they had paid for cherry trees to be planted. Today the trees remain and every spring the street is full of blossom.[27] Clara Brown cried when she saw the trees.

In her King's Cross Voices interview[28] Barbara Jacobson states that at the age of 19 she became a squatter in 25 Balfe Street. She had come from Berkeley, California, to study Japanese at the School of Oriental and African Studies. She says 'when I got here I found Thatcher had raised the student fees by a thoudand pounds, which was my rent budget, so that's how I ended up squatting. Out of necessity.'

Barbara lived with four others one of whom was Paul Lowenberg. 'It was certainly a step down for me in terms of technology. There was no heating, loo didn't work, just threw a bucket down it. Got showers and baths as we could. Norma was quite helpful with that. The house had several generations of electricity and fifteen layers of wallpaper and the old plaster was moving down. There were massive bulges over the skirting boards where the old plaster had fallen behind. The Council, i.e. the GLC, had originally wanted to knock Balfe Street down but partly as a result of a lot of work by Norma, Paul and others' (the others later including Islington Council) 'it was saved. The first political thing I was involved in was getting people to sign a petition to keep the houses in Balfe Street. It was basically down to Norma and her lobbying. I went and knocked on doors. People were very receptive, everybody signed and the street was saved.' In addition to these words Barbara wishes to add[29] that 'this was the first time I had heard the dismissive phrase, 'just throwing good money after bad'. It is something I heard again during a successful fight to save another swathe of run down council housing in Clerkenwell not far from Balfe Street.'

By 1980 Norma, her family and neighbours, felt, in Norma's words, that 'the community had achieved.'[30] Balfe Street had been saved but the campaigners rose to yet another challenge, to create the gardens that Stock Conversion had made provision for in Islington's Compulsory Purchase Order from them of all the houses in Balfe Street. These houses were the ones where Norma's family were now living, on the eastern side of the street. Between these houses, Wharfdale Road and Northdown Street (see next page) there was an empty space which was used as a

Top left: Residents campaign for a garden used as a car park. *Photo: Supplied by Norma Steel*
Bottom left: The car park as it was at the time of the campaign. *Photo: Supplied by Norma Steel*

Top right: Norma's mother, Clara, taking part in the garden campaign. *Photo: Supplied by Norma Steel*
Bottom right: Battlebridge Garden on the site of the former car park, June 2010. *Photo: Angela Inglis*

National Car Park. The house Norma had moved into in Northdown Street was beside the National Car Park Gates[31] and she and her neighbours set about persuading Islington Council to help them make this land into a garden. Norma says:[32] 'We had a tussle over this and in the end we squatted the car park. Originally we had hoped that this land could provide gardens for the rehabbed houses and flats. However, the money ran out and we pushed for the communal garden. We created lots of publicity.' They were successful and a garden was created by the early eighties. Norma and her neighbours called the completed garden Battlebridge Garden, echoing the old name for King's Cross and because they had had to fight so hard to achieve their aims. Photographs show this development at the time when Norma, her family and friends were finally able to enjoy the garden.

The Thornhill Neighbourhood Project Report for 1984/85[33] commented that 'It is intended that eventually the garden will be managed through joint arrangements between the Council and the residents of Balfe, Northdown and Wharfdale'. The report also states that 'the completion of nine new family houses and continued progress with the rehab programme in Balfe Street and Northdown Streets has brought a lot of new tenants to the area and created a feeling that things are looking up in this part of King's Cross. The Thornhill Neighbourhood Project has worked with residents through the King's Cross Working Party to closely monitor the rehab programme and to get action on a number of issues.'

In 1988 just as Norma, in Northdown Street, was enjoying the campaign's success she heard from Gordon Arnot[34] of the Thornhill Neighbourhood Project. 'He called me one day and said, "Norma, do you have a chair handy? I've got some rather horrific news." So I sat down. He said, "We have just found out that British Rail are looking to make King's Cross their Channel Tunnel terminal." I said, "Oh," it didn't really mean anything to me. Then he said, "It looks as if they are going to put the biggest hole Europe has ever seen smack bang in the middle of King's Cross." I just couldn't believe it. It was uncanny. It was absolutely devastating. After all the years of fighting for the community. It took a long time for the enormity of the project to sink in.' Norma continues, 'Everything changed then. The blight once again was on King's Cross'.

But being such a stalwart campaigner Norma and her family won through with another campaigning group. The story is told in the next chapter.

---

[1] Summer 2004 edition of Network magazine, Kings's Cross Railway Lands Group article by Leslie McCartney, 29th March, 2004

[2] As above

[3] Norma Steel's King's Cross Voices Interview with Leslie McCartney, 29th March, 2004

[4] Clara Brown's King's Cross Voices Interview with Leslie McCartney, 5th May, 2004

[5] Tunnel Vision, Why is British Rail Undermining Londoner's Lives? Paul Barker, Evening Standard, July1989

[6] As in [3] above

[7] Norma Steel in conversation with Angela Inglis, October 5th, 2010

[8] Norma's walk in Balfe Street with Angela Inglis and Martin Lipson, March 2nd, 2011

[9] As in [3] above

[10] Information provided by Paul Lowenberg in an email dated 13th June, 2010 See details about Paul Lowenberg later in this story

[11] Angela Inglis in conversation with Martin Lipson and Norma Steel, February 7th, 2010

[12] Norma Steel's King's Cross Voices Interview with Lesley McCartney, 29th March, 2004

[13] Document: Proof of Evidence of the King's Cross (Islington) Community Association to the Public Local Enquiry on the Battlebridge Basin Site at 15-16 New Wharf Road, N1 1974, as presented by Martin Lipson on behalf of the Community Association and his witness Anthony Rossi, member of the community Association committee of local residents. This paper is now lodged in the Archives at the Islington Local History Centre, Finsbury Library, 245 St John Street, London, EC4 4NB

[14] Above paper, page 5:15

[15] Above paper, page 6:17

[16] Above paper, page 6

[17] Council records

[18] Information provided by Lester Pritchard, October, 2011

[19] Angela Inglis in conversation with Paul Lowenberg, October 5th, 2010, and email confirming this information on 13th June, 2011

[20] Norma Steel's King's Cross Voices Interview with Lesley McCartney, 29th March, 2004

[21] Leader of the special Islington Planning Team in this particular period to deal with blighted areas

[22] Norma Steel in conversation with Angela Inglis, Oct 5th, 2010

[23] Paul Lowenberg's document sent to Angela Inglis, June 13th, 2011

[24] Thornhill Neighbourhood Project News Sheet dated March 1976 Archives Islington History Centre, Finsbury Library, 245 St John Street, London EC4 4NB

[25] Norma Steel's King's Cross Voices Interview with Leslie McCartney, 29th March 2004 and also confirmed in conversation with Angela Inglis on February 7th, 2011

[26] Norma in conversation with Angela Inglis, February 7th, 2011

[27] Norma in conversation with Angela Inglis, February 7th, 2011

[28] Barbara Jacobson in King's Cross Voices interview with Leslie McCartney, 7th June 2005

[29] Conversation with Angela Inglis, October 2011

[30] Norma's King's Cross Interview with Leslie McCartney, 29th March, 2004

[31] In conversation with Angela Inglis, February 7th, 2011

[32] Norma's King's Cross Interview as above

[33] Archives, Islington History Centre, Finsbury Library. Document L3332 947 Class No YB208 THOR

[34] Summer 2004 edition of Network magazine, King's Cross Railway Lands Group, article by Leslie McCartney

Appendix 1

History of Killick Street Health Centre

Pauline Nee
Photo: Angela Inglis

The Killick Street Health Centre was opened by Rupert Perry, Mayor of Islington, on 27th November, 1997, twenty years after the beginning of investigations by Pauline Nee into the provision of health care in the King's Cross neighbourhood. In 1977 she had been commissioned[1] to do this by the Thornhill Neighbourhood Project along with other workers who oversaw various local groups such as the King's Cross Community Association, Copenhagen Youth Club, the Barnsbury Tenants etc.

She began investigating the provision of doctors for the area and discovered there were twenty one. A good proportion of these were single handed practices, which was not considered to be the ideal way of serving a community. A third of the doctors were over 70 years of age and three of them over 80. These doctors were not keen on home visits or on visiting patients out of hours. The Area Health Authority provided one health worker who was assisted by a person on secondment from the London School of Hygiene. This, of course, was inadequate. Many of the people in this area were living in houses where calor gas and paraffin were the usual sources of heat; condensation was the result and created poor health conditions.

In the early eighties a campaign was put into being to create a health centre for the King's Cross Area. It had already been thought of in 1978.[2] It took another seventeen years, but it did come to fruition with the help of many local people. According to Norma Steel, Gordon Arnot[3] was a key campaigner for this clinic.

---

[1] Information from an interview with Pauline Nee July 2011

[2] Article in Islington Gazette 19.5.78 Thornhill warned of doctors on the go by Cleland Thom.

[3] Angela Inglis in conversation with Norma Steel, October 5th, 2010

Appendix 2

Mural at Killick Street Health Centre

Tiled mural by William De Morgan
Photo: Angela Inglis

This tiled wall panel of George III playing bowls on Copenhagen Fields, Islington, was discovered in 1997 by Mike Bruce, Conservation Initiatives Officer for Islington Council, behind a plywood covering in the Star and Garter, a derelict pub on the corner of Northdown Street and Caledonian Road, shortly before the building's reuse as an Islamic Education Centre. The then owner had started to try and remove the tiles and had done some damage. Mike Bruce asked him to stop and to remove the whole of the plywood cover. Only then did it become clear how good the panel was (later confirmed to be by William De Morgan).

The owner was happy to sell the panel so Mike Bruce attempted to find an alternative local site for it, and was delighted when the Health Authority agreed to have it for their new centre which was then being built. It was they who paid for its restoration by tile specialists at Ironbridge, and subsequently displayed it inside the Health Centre above the inner entrance.

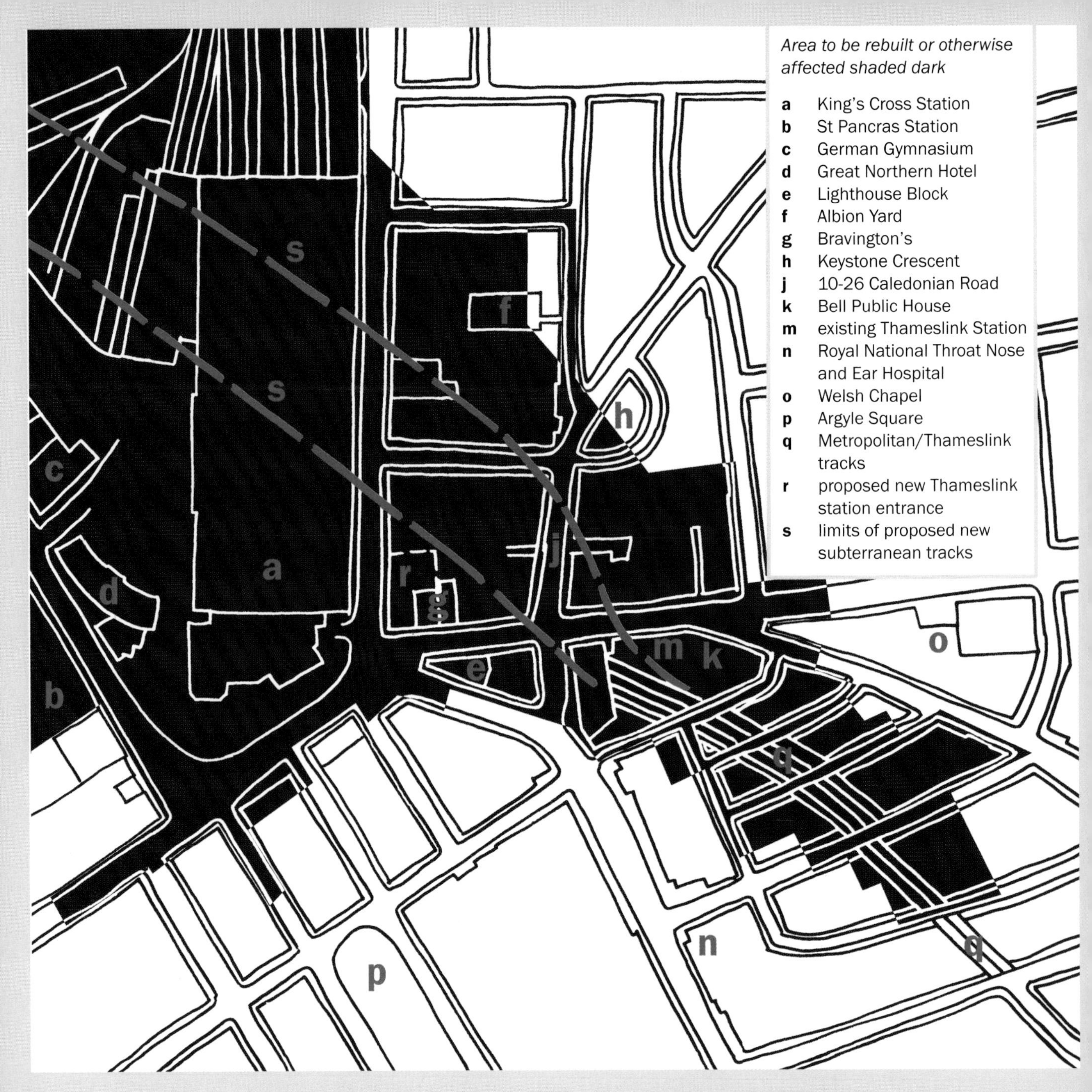

Land affected in King's Cross by British Rail plan c1989

Chapter 2

Railway threat, blight and survival

text and photographs by Randal Keynes

Introduction

This chapter is written by Randal Keynes who was living in Keystone Crescent in the South Cally area during the time of British Rail's project for an international station at King's Cross in the late 1980s and 1990s. The project would have involved demolition of four whole blocks of buildings in the streets immediately to the east of the station and the displacement of thousands of people who lived or worked there.

Throughout this period, many in the neighbourhood campaigned together against the plans, and they were finally successful in getting them dropped. As secretary of the South Caledonian Community Association and a member of the King's Cross Railway Lands Group, Randal joined forces with other key activists: Phil Jeffries (King's Cross Railway Lands Group), Aron Cronin (South Caledonian Community Association), Norma Steel of the local group Crossfire and Gordon Arnot of the Thornhill Neighbourhood Project. They were vigorously championed in Parliament by their MP Chris Smith and ably represented by local solicitor, David Harter.

It's a joy to walk down Caledonian Road today and south to the Scala knowing how the people who lived and worked here in the 1980s and 1990s helped to save these buildings and their heritage for future generations.

Angela Inglis

Map: A. Delarue

Left: York Way looking north from No. 16 to the Duke of York public house, corner of Caledonia Street.
Bottom: Railway Tavern, corner of Caledonia Street.
Photos: Late 1980s

Top: 10-14 York Way.
Bottom: Railway Street from York Way looking towards Balfe Street.
Photos: Late 1980s

Railway threat, blight and survival

Arrival and impressions

I came to live in South Cally in 1986 because I'd seen Keystone Crescent and just wanted to live there. I liked the contrasts of the area: the crowds of travellers moving between train, bus and tube and the sudden change to quietness in the narrow streets around. The neighbourhood was part of the small pocket of King's Cross between the station to the west, Regent's Canal to the north, Pentonville Road to the south and Killick Street to the east (see map page 14). The shops were diverse – an Italian deli, Housmans Bookshop, porn shops, an aquarium shop, a hardware store, an oculist and a hairdresser's, and the people living and working there included Scots shopkeepers, an Irish publican, Bangladeshis, Turkish and Greek Cypriots and a Sri Lankan poet. Some of the oldest were Italians who had come in the 1930s, while many of the most recent arrivals were young and middle-aged professionals like me.

We couldn't be sentimental about the neighbourhood, with the crowds coming to and from the station, the winos, sex workers and drug dealers. The pavements were strewn with litter, dropped take-aways and spilt drink, urine and vomit. There was almost no open space for children to play; the only greenery was the buddleia along the cracks in the rooftops. But many people along the side streets knew each other well, and we all got on, partly because there was no point in anyone setting themselves apart from anyone else, but often also with the neighbourliness that is the special benefit of many places like South Cally in run-down parts of London.

Railway Lands and Low Level Station

All activity in the area and all plans for its development depended on King's Cross Station with St Pancras alongside and the extensive King's Cross Railway Lands to the north, formerly a major goods yard but now almost empty and underused. In the London commercial property boom of the mid-1980s, British Rail saw the Railway Lands as an obvious opportunity for commercial development following their success with their Broadgate development next to Liverpool Street Station, and in 1987 the British Railways Property Board launched an ambitious plan for a major

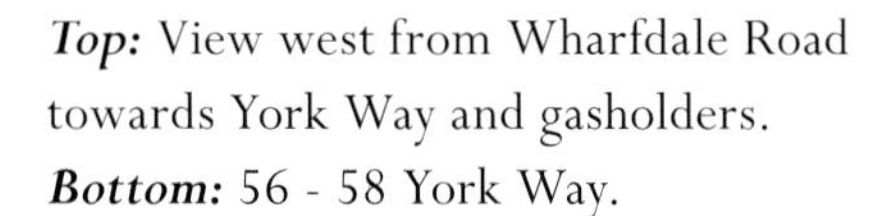

Top: View west from Wharfdale Road towards York Way and gasholders.
Bottom: 56 - 58 York Way.
Photos: Late 1980s

Above: Lincoln Arms public house and 54 York Way.
Photo: Late 1980s

development with a commercial partner, opening a project office in the Railway Lands to work up the plan and find their partner.

There was also another opportunity to consider at the time. The Channel Tunnel was being built and when it was opened in 1994 it would enable rail services to be run from London to Paris and Brussels. In the first years the trains would use existing lines from Waterloo, but capacity and speeds would be limited. For the future, British Rail were planning a dedicated high-speed line, the Channel Tunnel Rail Link (CTRL), possibly with a new London station for through services to the north. They realised that if they could get the high-speed line to King's Cross and put the new station somewhere there while leaving enough of the Railway Lands free for office development, they'd be able to raise the commercial value of the whole venture to a very high figure. When they worked out where they might be able to fit the new station in, they found that in order to leave enough of their property clear for a high profit on the office development, they would have to position the new station below ground with a large part beneath King's Cross Station and another large part beneath what were then other people's properties to the south and east. They'd have to obtain those properties by compulsory purchase, demolish them, dig out the space for the station, construct the station and then roof it over for replacement buildings from ground level up.

Seeing the potential for a huge profit from the Railway Lands development if they could start on the new station at once, British Rail quickly worked up their proposal for it, even though they had not yet worked out any corresponding plan for the high-speed line they'd have to tunnel through south and central London to reach it. They called it the Low Level Station and added it into their project plans for the Railway Lands development so that they could carry on with the project without delay.[1] They kept the plan secret from local people but revealed it to the developers they had invited to tender for the Railway Lands scheme so that the developers could cover it in their proposals. During the summer of 1987 one developer showed a map for its proposal to some local people and left in by mistake the lines British Rail had provided for the Low Level Station. Someone asked what the lines were and the secret was out. News spread fast and when people pressed the Railway Lands

Top: Northdown Street looking south towards Caledonian Road.
Bottom: 46 and 48 Caledonian Road and looking into Keystone Crescent.
Photos: Late 1980s

Top: Keystone Crescent.
Bottom: Caledonian Road at corner with Keystone Crescent.
Photos: Late 1980s

project staff, they confirmed that they were considering adding a station for the CTRL to their scheme, and admitted that their plan for the Low Level Station would involve taking over some properties in South Cally and demolishing them for the construction works.

Local groups and campaigns

When local people had first learnt about the Railway Lands project, a number had come together and formed the King's Cross Railway Lands Community Development Group to find out about the proposals and work out how they could possibly influence the development for the benefit of all like them who were living and working around the site.[2] As soon as the Railway Lands Group discovered about the plan for the Low Level Station, it realised how closely the two projects were linked with each other and saw that British Rail were developing them together as two parts of a single overall scheme. From then on the Railway Lands Group treated them itself in that way, focusing now on one, now on the other, and now on the scheme as a whole.

After the days of the King's Cross Community Association in the 1970s and early 1980s (see map page 14), there were now two community organizations active in South Cally, Crossfire and the South Caledonian Community Association (SCCA). Both were represented in Islington Council's Neighbourhood Forum for the area, Crossfire speaking mainly for tenants in the Council housing and SCCA speaking for the private tenants and owner/occupiers. I was secretary of SCCA, and the Council-funded Thornhill Neighbourhood Project led by Gordon Arnot (see photo page 18) was still working hard for us all. When we learnt what British Rail was planning to do to South Cally in constructing the Low Level Station, Gordon talked at once with Crossfire and SCCA, and we joined with the Railway Lands Group to plan a combined campaign. Through the six years we all had to deal with the Low Level Station, we cooperated closely, each speaking now for one of the organizations and now for another according to the needs of the moment. We were a very mixed group of people with many different interests, backgrounds and contributions to make. We worked well together with Phil Jeffries playing a key role as one of the leaders of the Railway Lands Group.

Above: Kings Cross Aquarium, Caledonian Road, corner with Omega Place.
Photos: Late 1980s

Top: Kings X Greengrocers, Caledonian Road.
Bottom: Café, Caledonian Road.
Photos: Late 1980s

Plan and impact

In December 1987 British Rail produced an information booklet for their project for the Low Level Station with a map indicating all the properties they intended to take for the works.[3] It was a jarring shock for us to see their view of our streets and buildings and to find that we, the people living and working there, weren't mentioned. The buildings they planned to take from us and demolish were shown simply as "Land to be acquired" with no reference at all to the many hundreds of people who'd lose their homes or workplaces.

It was soon worked out that British Rail was planning to take seventeen acres of property from the streets immediately east and south east of the station. All the buildings would be demolished and the site would be excavated to a depth of 40 feet for the construction of the station and rebuilding above. British Rail eventually had to admit the extent of the destruction. 150 buildings in all would be demolished, including 88 homes and 168 workplaces, among them 59 local shops of which 38 provided key services. 326 people would lose their homes and 1,620 local jobs would be lost.[4] For those who'd stay in the surrounding area, the whole project would take six years to complete with working up to seven days a week and 24 hours a day when required. The effects on us would often be unbearable because the demolition, excavation and construction would be taking place directly next door to our homes and workplaces.

British Rail's approach to the building of this new station followed the ruthless methods railway companies had been able to use in the nineteenth century when they brought their lines into central London through the crowded slums of the Victorian city. Charles Dickens had seen their bulldozing through Camden in the 1830s for the railway to Euston Station and wrote about it with fierce irony in his novel *Dombey and Son:*

> The first shock of a great earthquake had, just at that period, rent the whole neighbourhood to its centre... Everywhere were bridges that led nowhere; thoroughfares that were wholly impassable; Babel towers of chimneys, wanting half their height; temporary wooden houses and enclosures, in the most unlikely situations; carcases of ragged tenements,

Above: Phil Jeffries, 2006. *Photo: Diana Shelley*

Top: Lord Chris Smith, 2011. *Photo: Angela Inglis*
Bottom: David Harter, 2010. *Photo: Angela Inglis*

> and fragments of unfinished walls and arches, and piles of scaffolding, and wildernesses of bricks, and giant forms of cranes, and tripods straddling above nothing ... In short, the yet unfinished and unopened Railroad was in progress; and, from the very core of all this dire disorder, trailed smoothly away, upon its mighty course of civilisation and improvement.[5]

The last times before now that this kind of railway building had been carried out in London had been in the 1890s with the demolition of many properties for Marylebone Station and in the 1900s when a disreputable neighbourhood next to Waterloo Station known as 'Whoreterloo' was cleared for enlargement of the station.[6] Since then, no stations or railways had been built on this scale, destroying so many close-packed inner city premises so close to others where people would be trying to carry on living and working and would have to survive as they could in the noise and dirt of the works immediately around them. Eighty years on, British Rail now clearly felt they had another opportunity to clear a worthless area of inner city decay for a major railway and commercial development in today's "mighty course of civilisation and improvement", and trusted that everyone with any sense would see their plan as a great benefit to London and the nation. They appeared to believe that anyone living or working in the areas to be cleared should be happy to leave for the clearance and rebuilding, and any who weren't could be disregarded as flies on the windscreen of progress.

When news of British Rail's plans first spread in South Cally, we all agreed at once that the first need was to support and protect our local shops. In our streets, as well as providing all the goods they stocked, the shops were our main places for meeting and talking with each other. If an elderly person needed help, one of the shopkeepers would often be the first to notice and alert a neighbour. Eight of the shops in a parade from 10 to 24 Caledonian Road were owned by Derek Stuckey whose family have owned them for generations, and he was happy to keep his rents low for shopkeepers who were providing essential services for people in the neighbourhood. British Rail planned to demolish 27 of the shops including seven food stores, two newsagents, two bicycle shops and the hairdresser's. They clearly had no idea of the shops' importance for all who lived and worked in South Cally and how the neighbourhood would be drained of life if they were removed. SCCA gave the shopkeepers clip-boards with a letter to sign and in a few days we had 336 signatures from their customers.[7]

Parliament and petitioning

Faced with the boldness of British Rail's plan, we quickly recognised that our accustomed ways of campaigning on community issues – neighbourhood action, lobbying Ward Councillors and Council staff and pressure at Council meetings - would be useless for the campaign we'd have to mount. But British Rail's need for special powers of compulsory purchase to acquire our properties for the works and the special requirements for granting those powers would give us other opportunities. They'd have to deposit a private bill in Parliament for approval by the Commons and the Lords; our MP Chris Smith could act for us in the Commons; we could hope to find peers to support us in the Lords; we'd be able to make formal petitions to both Houses on the bill and in each House's committee hearings on it we'd be able to question British Rail's witnesses on their claims for their proposals and then make our own cases against them.

When we first learnt about all this, we had no idea what we might be able to achieve by using these rights, but some among us with experience of campaigning on other issues suggested that we should find out about our powers and see what we could do with them. As soon as Chris Smith heard about British Rail's plans, he saw clearly the terrible threat they presented to all his constituents in South Cally. He came at once to hear what we were finding out from British Rail and others about what lay ahead, and agreed with us what he could do to help us.

British Rail drew up their King's Cross Railways Bill for the station works and the powers they'd need to carry them out, and deposited it in Parliament on 29 November 1988.[8] The owners of all properties subject to compulsory purchase were then informed, and notices appeared in local newspapers with information about the deadline for petitioning. Both Islington and Camden Councils had strong concerns about British Rail's proposals and lodged petitions on their points. The wording of a petition had to follow a number of elaborate formulae. The Railway Lands Group and the Thornhill Neighbourhood Project obtained all the obligatory phrases from the

Commons Private Bill Office; we composed a basic text on our Amstrad microcomputers; we drew up three main petitions for the Railway Lands Group, Crossfire and SCCA, and we held petitioning workshops to draw up individual petitions for everyone who wanted to lodge their own.

Some of those who would lose their premises were fatalistic about what British Rail was planning to inflict on them. One of the shopkeepers, Kate Kerr, had just stocked her small shop for household goods and toiletries with her four years' savings as a secretary and now realised that she'd lose the shop without compensation for the stock as soon as British Rail started their work. At first she saw no point in bothering to petition as she felt that what she was facing was something that any ordinary person in a position like ours just had to accept whenever "the big people" decided to bulldoze them. After hearing from us how she could make her case directly to Parliament, she explained her points to us and we produced a petition for her setting them out as she wanted.

282 petitions against the bill were delivered to the House of Commons.[9] That was at that time a new record for Parliament. British Rail challenged many of them and a number were disallowed, but 151 were accepted for the Committee to consider.

Commons debate and Committee

The full Parliamentary procedure for dealing with a private bill like the King's Cross Railways Bill has three main stages in the Commons which are then repeated in the Lords. After the promoters have deposited the bill, they find an MP to act as sponsor for it in the Commons; he asks for a first debate known as Second Reading; after the debate a Committee of MPs is appointed to consider the overall purpose of the bill and its detailed provisions, and reports to the House; the sponsor then asks for a second debate known as Third Reading and that debate ends with the House's decision whether to approve the bill. If the bill is approved, the promoters find a sponsor in the Lords; he asks for Second Reading there; a Committee of Peers is appointed to consider the bill and reports; the sponsor asks for Third Reading and if the bill is approved by the Lords, it is finally passed to become an Act of Parliament with statutory force.

Second Reading in the Commons took place on 8 May 1989.[10] The bill's sponsor, Sir George Young MP, spoke first, setting out British Rail's case for the station at King's Cross and the powers they were seeking to build it. Chris Smith spoke next as MP for the constituency most severely affected. He told the House that British Rail's plan involved nothing less than the "massive destruction of a thriving local neighbourhood". He pointed to the difficulty the House would have in judging whether the proposal for the station was sound, because, absurdly, British Rail had not yet produced a plan for the line that would bring trains to the station, and it would obviously be impossible for the Commons to judge the need for the station and the soundness of the plan for it with no route yet planned or costed for Government approval and with no advice on the strategic framework for the whole project. There were serious questions about the Government's preparedness to fund the project, and the Government "must come clean on financing". Chris was supported by a number of MPs who were concerned about the possible route of the line through Kent and London but the Government spokesman and MPs for northern constituencies welcomed the bill and it was voted through to the Committee stage. Despite most MPs' confidence in British Rail, all Chris's key points turned out to be fully justified by the facts as they gradually emerged in the following years.

Neil Hamilton was appointed to chair the Commons Committee on the bill and three other MPs were appointed to make up the membership. They held their hearings in the House's Grand Committee Room.[11] British Rail's legal team was led by a QC in a wig and gown with a team of assistants with boxes of flagged documents. Beside them sat the petitioners' advocates, first the QC for Islington and Camden Councils with his team and then David Harter, Phil Jeffries and Aron Cronin representing between them the Railway Lands Group, Crossfire, SCCA and many individual petitioners.

The QC for British Rail put their case for the bill and called their expert witnesses to provide evidence. The petitioners' advocates could then cross-examine them, and the Committee then asked its questions. David Harter and Phil Jeffries' first achievements for us were to reveal a number of faults in British Rail's case caused by their rush to get the bill enacted in time to be able to profit from the Railway Lands development. Phil had probed British Rail's engineering case for flaws in their plans and had found a number. David Harter then teased them out for the Committee in careful and patient cross-examination of British Rail's expert witnesses, with a never-failing good humour that the Committee came to enjoy. Whenever he started on another point that might take an entertaining turn, one of the members could be seen to prick up his ears and shuffle his constituency mail back under his Committee papers in order to concentrate on what was being said. One day as they came back into the Committee room after lunch, he asked David, 'Any hand-grenades to throw in this afternoon?'

The most serious problem for British Rail emerged towards the end of its evidence. Phil Jeffries had worked out that the station platforms, each almost a quarter of a mile long, were still too short for the eighteen-coach trains; David drew out the point in cross-examination and the audience could all imagine an ever-repeated warning to passengers each time a Channel Tunnel train drew in to the station, that "the doors in the last carriage will not open". British Rail witnesses tried for four days to conceal the error and its significance in a hopeless effort to escape having to make a procedural concession they were determined to avoid if they could. At the final point Mr Hamilton suddenly revealed his exasperation with them by throwing his pencil at the water jug, an extraordinary moment in the rigorously calm politeness of the Committee's proceedings.

When the time came for the petitioners to make their points, the QC for Islington and Camden Councils led for us all on the transport issues that would arise with the fifteen million more travellers each year expected to pass through the station. He also explained the severe impacts of the clearance and construction works on the Council tenants and others who'd be living and working immediately next to them. David Harter and other advocates helped petitioners and other witnesses to explain to the Committee how the works would affect their lives for the six years they'd take.

There were many elderly people living in the affected area, some of whom had been there since before the Second World War. Norma Steel explained to the Committee how her elderly mother and her bed-ridden mother-in-law each lived on their own in a street across which they'd directly face the huge excavation. Their GP's surgery would be on the far side of the whole construction site. If the works were carried out, they'd also lose the local oculist who helped the elderly and infirm greatly by making home visits, as his premises would be demolished. Norma spoke strongly about the effect the works would have on her elderly neighbours and herself. "Everything we're used to is just going to go. It is going to completely destroy our whole lives."

Other witnesses for SCCA gave evidence about the loss of our local shops. The shopkeepers who would lose their premises explained how difficult it would be for them to find other premises nearby where they could carry on trading. Compensation for their tenancies would be low and they couldn't hope to attract in any of the replacement premises that might be available the local custom they'd need to cover the rents they'd have to pay. British Rail were offering compensation at statutory rates and were trying to be generous on a few points, but they didn't have the understanding of the neighbourhood's low-rent, low-income patterns of shopkeeping that was required to appreciate what kinds of help the shopkeepers would need. David Harter and his witnesses set out this whole problem for the Committee to explain to them how much our small inner-city community depended on the very low-cost local shopping services we were lucky to have. The shopkeepers that could remain in the neighbourhood would only be able to stay open during the six years of the works if they were given considerable help, and if they had to close and leave, many of their customers would not be able to continue living there without them.

Kate Kerr, the shopkeeper who at first had not felt it was worth petitioning, was now eager to give evidence to the Committee about the information British Rail had given her when she first heard about the possibility that she'd lose her shop. A British Rail spokesman had answered her anxious enquiry with an assurance that her premises would not be affected and she was upset to find out later after she'd spent her savings to stock the shop that they would be. British Rail's QC tried to persuade her in patronising cross-examination that she must have misunderstood the spokesman, but she insisted that the Committee should hear what she clearly remembered he'd told her.

The Committee had to listen to 51 days of arguments and evidence in its public hearings before it could report. This total had only ever been exceeded before in private bill proceedings when the Committee hearings on the historic bill in 1834 for the Great Western Railway from London to Bristol ran to 57 days.[12] Our Committee took so long to deal with the single station at King's Cross mainly because of the flaws and tangles in British Rail's case for it and the way they'd put the case forward before they had a route for the line to the station. This was shown most clearly in the last few days of the proceedings. Just as the Committee was preparing its report, the Secretary of State for Transport, then Cecil Parkinson, made an announcement about the whole project for the CTRL for which the Low Level Station would be the London terminus, which took the Committee by surprise. It emerged that British Rail had at last drawn up a plan for the line to the station and put it to Mr Parkinson for approval. To reach the point of entry to the Low Level Station, British Rail proposed to bring the line to the station in a tunnel through south and central London, but the cost would be far higher that the rough figure they'd guessed before they first presented their plan for the station to the Department for Transport. Mr Parkinson had to announce that the Government could not provide the £1.9 billion of cash and loans British Rail were now requesting for the line in addition to the £830 million they'd said they would need for the station. The Department for Transport had explained to British Rail the strict limits on what funding could be provided and had asked them to examine and report on other options, especially one for an eastern route that might be significantly less costly than British Rail's southern route and would have regional planning benefits for Essex and East London with which the southern route would have none to compare.

Many commentators on railway planning could see at once that this decision to change the route of the line to King's Cross from a southerly approach to one from the east, opened up possibilities for the CTRL to use an overground line to the station and for the station at King's Cross to be somewhere above ground, and there might be considerable savings in any options for the route and the station that could use those two opportunities together. At that time, the Department of Transport chose not to recognise the possibility for the station and Mr Parkinson simply said about the switch to an easterly route while sticking with the planned station for a line from the south, that "In our view, nothing in this statement invalidates the benefits to British Rail of the House proceeding with the King's Cross Railways Bill."[13] The Committee and others understood this at the time to be an assurance of Government support for British Rail's Low Level Station. With hindsight it can now be seen that in talking solely about "the benefits to British Rail" Mr Parkinson was in fact carefully avoiding any such assurance.

The Committee finally reported on 26 June 1990.[14] They wrote that they were clear about the value of the CTRL for the nation but they also recognised the terrible impact of British Rail's plan for the station on local people. They found themselves in a very difficult position for judging the purpose of the bill and complained both about the uncertainties about British Rail's plans and about the Government's position. "We consider that the net effect of the Secretary of State's announcement is not to dispel but to perpetuate the uncertainties which have surrounded the route and financing of the Channel Tunnel Link." They noted that it was an established principle of private bill procedure that a bill should only be approved and enacted if it was clear that the promoters had the funds needed to carry out the works. They decided that in their difficult position, they had to approve the principle of the bill but declared that they were only prepared to recommend proceeding with it on a firm understanding that British Rail was now working on fresh proposals for the route and arrangements for financing them, and as long as the Lords Committee on the bill would be able to satisfy itself about the viability of British Rail's proposals for the station when the plan for the route was eventually settled, and then obtain clear assurances from the Government on the availability of the funding required.

The Committee strongly criticised British Rail's conduct during the proceedings, pointing out that at one critical stage they'd used lobbying tactics to try to get the bill through that "verged on being a contempt of Parliament", and Chris Smith commented to The Guardian, "I'm glad that the Committee have given British Rail a roasting."[15]

Delay and Third Reading

British Rail had hoped to be able to get the bill approved by the Commons and taken through the Lords for their approval and enactment by the end of 1990, but with the Government's rejection of their proposal for the line and its instruction to them to review and report on options for the eastern route, the CTRL and Low Level Station projects were now both under question until the options could be examined and proposals decided on. British Rail decided they had to wait until they had a plan for the line that the Government would be prepared to assure Parliament it would fund before they could ask for the final Commons debate and the House's approval of the bill.

We had to wait until autumn 1991, sixteen months later, for British Rail to make their recommendations for the eastern route and for the Secretary of State for Transport, now Malcolm Rifkind, to decide on them. Mr Rifkind announced on 14 October that British Rail had reported on the options for the eastern route that the Government had asked for in June 1990.[16] Mr Rifkind had decided that the eastern route should be adopted for all further work. He'd instructed British Rail to form a subsidiary, Union Railways, to take responsibility for the CTRL and work up a detailed plan for the easterly route and next steps. On the Low Level Station at King's Cross, he announced that British Rail had kept their plan for the Low Level Station in their recommendations for the eastern route. He left it for them to work out how to tunnel the new line from the east underground to the south of King's Cross in order to reach the required position for the lines in to the Low Level Station.

Faced with British Rail's persistence in pressing for the Low Level Station and the Government's repeated acceptance of it without any indication that it had been established to be affordable, we realised at this point that the process of working out the route to the station and establishing whether the Government would be prepared to provide the funding needed for it might drag on for many more years. We were now in a second crisis for South Cally as the neighbourhood was being engulfed in a wave of street crime in which the emptying and decay of our buildings due to the blight they lay under because of the King's Cross Railways Bill was certainly a factor. We had to rethink our approach to saving South Cally because if we just continued to wait for a sound decision on the CTRL and where to put the station that the Government was prepared to underwrite with funding,

Left and right: Premises empty in 1993.

our community might be undermined by the urban decay and overcome by the crime wave before the decision was reached.

King's Cross, like areas around many city railway stations, had always been a convenient neighbourhood for casual criminal dealings and prostitution, with easy access and anonymity for casual contacts with strangers. Householders in Keystone Crescent couldn't count it a surprise when in 1989 one couple placed their house with a letting agency for a few months away and found on coming back that "VICE GANG FILLED OUR HOME WITH CALL-GIRLS" as *The People* headlined its report. On their return the horrified couple "discovered that their listed Victorian house had TWO extra phones to take constant calls from punters, and EXPENSIVE video cameras for making porn movies."[17]

Our streets had now been blighted since 1987 by British Rail's plan for the Low Level Station and its lodging the bill for the powers to obtain all the properties it needed by compulsory purchase. Since then, any improvements would have been pointless; many landlords were now aiming for vacant possession, not occupancy, and premises were being emptied and boarded up every month. During 1991 the whole area south and east of King's Cross Station was hit by a flare-up of drug-dealing and prostitution which quickly made King's Cross a national byword for inner city squalor and criminality. Prostitutes served clients and drug addicts got their fixes in our basement areas. My wife would bring our two small children home from nursery school past suppliers doing deals with customers in the alley-ways. One feature of the drug-dealing in those years was the numbers of young Italians who came to London and King's Cross with needs for heroin or crack cocaine. One or two came to the Italian stores in our neighbourhood when they were in great difficulties and asked for help. One of the shopkeepers did what he could for them but still remembers one young addict who died in a bedsit in Kentish Town beyond any help he could give.

The street-crime grew so bad by March 1991 that the Metropolitan Police set up Operation Welwyn, a dedicated specialist street crime unit, to cope with the area. And then in October, the Government's Director of Public Prosecutions no less, was arrested by the police kerb-crawling along Goods

Above: Omega Place, 1991.

Top: Goods Way, 1991.
Bottom: New Wharf Road, 1993.

Way, the best-known street for "business" around the station. Shortly after, a spray-painter scrawled along the street wall, "The DPP crawled here". For us, petitioning Parliament for this neighbourhood as we were, the situation was absurd.

We now saw that the Government might possibly allow the King's Cross Railways Bill to be approved by Parliament and enacted but still have no intention of providing the money, and be happy if the whole Rail Link project were delayed indefinitely with the impasse over the costs and available funding. If the bill was enacted but the station works were then stalled because of lack of funds, South Cally would be blighted by the Act for the indefinite future, and as the neighbourhood continued to decay it would eventually become impossible to save our streets as an area where anyone could be happy to live and work. We decided we should aim to force British Rail and the Government to own up to Parliament that the Low Level Station project was unfundable, and do all we could to assist any efforts to identify any alternatives that might be fundable, so that the Low Level Station could be rejected and the bill withdrawn simply because there was another better option that could be adopted, funded and built.

With Mr Rifkind's support for the Low Level Station in his October 1991 statement, British Rail at last reckoned that it could safely ask for Commons approval of the bill and requested Third Reading for their final decision. We set to work on the costs and funding and wrote to the Minister for Transport, Roger Freeman, asking for the latest figures for Chris Smith to be able to refer to in the debate. An official replied on Mr Freeman's behalf that British Rail had not yet provided any costing or investment case for the scheme it was now planning to propose, and therefore, as things stood then, the Department couldn't say whether British Rail's proposal would be acceptable.[18] The Third Reading debate was held on 28 January 1992[19] and Chris went straight to the point. "Not only do we not have in front of us an exact cost for the works that are being voted through in this bill... but the Government are saying that they do not have the foggiest idea whether the amount involved will accord with their investment criteria." Mr Freeman could only say in reply: "It is not possible to come to a firm conclusion about this project in financial terms at the moment." A majority of MPs trusted that British Rail's plans were sound and the Government would be able to provide the funds needed, and the Commons approved the bill, 165 votes to 5, for passing on to the Lords.

Lords debate and Committee

The bill arrived in the Lords in early February, but again, to our surprise, nothing happened. British Rail was having another problem with the Government about funding. It emerged in April that the Government had not given British Rail enough funding for 1992 for them to be able to include the CTRL and the Low Level Station in their work programme for the year. British Rail told journalists they were putting the two projects in a separate list and would "lobby hard" for the sums they needed.[20]

Shortly after, we heard that British Rail had managed to persuade Lord Whitelaw to sponsor the bill in the Lords, a great advantage for them with the general goodwill towards him in the House. We produced a detailed report, "King's Cross Project – costs and financial viability"[21] setting out all that was known about the cost of the works, the funding that would be needed from the Government and what they were prepared to provide. We concluded that as far as could be determined, British Rail would have to ask the Government for grants and loans of up to £1 billion or more and it was quite possible that the Government would have to refuse. We sent copies of the report to British Rail, the Department for Transport and the Treasury, inviting them to let us know about any figures that we'd got wrong or points we'd missed. We gave our conclusions to *The Times* which reported them for Peers to read in their newspapers and Whitehall officials to note in their daily press cuttings.[22] There was no response from British Rail or the Department of Transport but we were encouraged when the Head of Public Expenditure at the Treasury wrote to thank us for our analysis, saying "I have read the paper with care and found it very interesting. It is helpful of you to send it to me".[23]

We approached a number of Peers with our concerns, our information about the issues and some suggestions for the Second Reading debate before the Lords Committee's hearings. They all listened carefully, recognised our concerns and offered to help us. The debate was held on 1 June.[24] Five Peers spoke in the debate about the issues we'd put to them, suggesting points to be borne in mind by the Committee on the bill. Lord Rea, a North

London GP, spoke first emphasizing the need for the House to check that the Government would be prepared to fund the works before enacting the bill. Lady David, an active Labour Peer, said she had come to South Cally to meet people from the area whose premises would be destroyed. She commented that "the community spirit, of which I was very much aware, will be destroyed too", and declared her support for Lord Rea's points.

Lord Henderson, former Clerk to the House of Lords who was a highly respected authority on issues of Parliamentary principle, had been shocked to read the harsh criticisms the Commons Committee had felt it had to make of British Rail's conduct in the Commons; he took up the Commons Committee's recommendation on the need for the Lords to check that funding was assured, explaining that it was an important principle for the proper use of Parliamentary powers.[25] He referred to our report which showed that there was no certainty about Government willingness to fund the works, and declared "I urge the Committee when it considers the bill, and the House when the bill returns to it, to ensure that they have cast iron guarantees from the promoters and from the Government. Nothing less will do than the approval of the Department of Transport and the Treasury to the money being forthcoming. That guarantee will be sufficient; nothing else will do."

Lord Caithness, the Minister for Transport in the Lords, declared the Government's support for the bill. He referred to Lord Rea and Lord Henderson's comments on the financial issue but could only reply lamely that the Government could not provide assurances on the financing of such projects before the final go-ahead of the project because figures might always change. He had asked for "updated financial information" and had looked at the figures provided. He commented that "nothing we have seen so far causes us to query British Rail's judgment that the station works should meet our normal investment criteria". This point was an irrelevance mentioned only to avoid the real concern. The investment criteria are simply rules for calculations of a rate of return required on any Government investment. The essential question about funding was whether the Government had the amount available and was prepared to provide it for that purpose, an entirely separate and far tougher issue.

Five Peers were appointed to the Committee on the bill, with Lord Greenhill, a former head of the Diplomatic Service, as Chairman. They held seventeen days of hearings on the bill, at which British Rail made their case for the Low Level Station, insisting that it was the best option and there should be no difficulty in getting it funded.[26] Disregarding the Treasury's primary authority in Whitehall decisions on public spending, the QC for British Rail suggested that it would be good for the Lords to approve the bill at that point ahead of the Government's decision on public funding for the scheme "because such a decision will be the impetus for a Government decision on funding the scheme". She made it clear that she meant by that a decision "to fund the scheme", not "whether to", when she went on to comment that "a favourable decision on the bill will be the impetus for early implementation". British Rail was now asking Parliament to enact its private bill in order to put political pressure on the Government to agree to fund the proposed works. This was either brazen or naïve. British Rail simply didn't see how improper the suggestion was and how ineffective it would be as long as the Treasury would have to insist that the amounts wanted were not available.

In his case to the Committee for us, David Harter explained the impacts of the works on our neighbourhood, and then focused our challenge on the cost of the works, whether the Treasury would allow the Department of Transport to fund them, and the consequences for the whole neighbourhood if the bill was enacted but not implemented as a result of funding not being provided. Helpfully for what happened later, he explained how you could check what public funding any major project had for three years ahead by looking at the Government's provision for it in its annual Public Expenditure Survey. If there was no provision in the annual statement it was highly unlikely that any would be obtainable later.

The Lords Committee made their report on the bill in July 1992.[27] They acknowledged all the points that were most important to us and stated that in judging the bill they had "weighed the advantages the bill would bring against the savage local impact of the scheme in human and material terms during construction". They were also clearly concerned about the damage the neighbourhood had already suffered from the years of blight inflicted by the bill and said they "did accept the petitioners' argument that it would be wrong for us to pass the bill if we were not satisfied that the powers it bestowed would be used". On our key concern about funding, they followed the Commons Committee's lead and declared firmly that they "would consider it wrong of the Government to fail to clarify the future availability of funds as soon as the scheme is finally presented for approval" and suggested that the Minister should "make a statement of intent during the Third Reading of the bill".

St Pancras and final decisions

During 1992, while the King's Cross Railways Bill was in the Lords, Union Railways were working on the plan for the eastern route that Mr Rifkind had asked for in October 1991. They and other British Rail experts were considering the financial problems for all aspects of the CTRL and, aware of the tight constraints the Government was placing on public funding, they were looking for ways to keep costs to an absolute minimum. Looking at the Low Level Station, they now recognised both the very high cost of construction with the central part of the station having to be put together immediately beneath a functioning mainline railway station that was also a Grade 1 Listed building, and the extra cost of having to tunnel the line to it from the south through central London in order to come in at the right place. They saw possible savings by putting the station on the surface somewhere else in the Railway Lands, with use of St Pancras the obvious first option to consider, and also by avoiding the expense of having to tunnel the final part of the line into central London to come into the Low Level Station from the south east at a point itself south east of King's Cross. A group in Union Railways started work on a plan for St Pancras, seeing how exciting a "St Pancras International" might be and how welcome it might be to the Department for Transport as a more affordable solution for the London terminus of the CTRL.[28]

We learnt about the group's work only after the Lords Committee had reported, and we heard then also that their proposal was not welcomed by senior management in British Rail who still believed that if only they could get the King's Cross Railways Bill enacted, they could force the Government to provide the full funding needed for their original plan.

In October 1992 we were in touch with Lord Henderson and he was in touch with Lord Whitelaw who told him that British Rail was pressing him to ask for Third Reading.[29] After the Lords Committee's report on the bill, Lord Henderson was now determined to ensure that the bill should only be approved by the House if the Government was prepared to provide a clear assurance that it would be prepared to fund the works. He told us that he'd spoken to Lord Whitelaw and Lord Caithness about the matter and had made it clear to them that if Lord Whitelaw asked for Third Reading, he'd speak in the debate and ask Lord Caithness clearly and firmly for the assurance the two Committees had said would be needed before the bill could be approved. If Lord Caithness could not provide it, he'd then argue on Parliamentary principle that the bill should not be approved.

At that time we were also in touch with officials in the Department of Transport and indirectly with contacts in Union Railways. We told Lord Henderson that Department of Transport officials were indicating to us that there was no funding for the Low Level Station. We told both the Department and him what we were gathering about the St Pancras option. The Department was aware of the option, whether from its proponents in Union Railways or only its opponents in British Rail we didn't know. Lord Henderson asked two Parliamentary Questions about the financing of the CTRL and the Low Level Station to check what Lord Caithness might be prepared to say about the station in the House if pressed in a debate. Lord Caithness's replies showed that there was no money for construction in the three years ahead, and it was stated that "no undertakings or statements have been made to British Rail in relation to funding for these projects after 1995/96".[30]

Shortly before Christmas, Union Railways delivered its report on the CTRL and the Low Level Station to British Rail senior management. It explained the possibility of putting the station in St Pancras and noted that option would be significantly cheaper. The Board met and decided to instruct Union Railways to revise its report as the Board was not prepared to recommend the St Pancras option to the Government but wanted to put its case for the Low Level Station first. Remarkably, it then briefed the transport correspondent of *The Independent* about the decision, presumably to prepare the ground for making their case for the Low Level Station to the Government, and he duly reported it in the newspaper on 23 December.[31]

British Rail delivered Union Railways' revised report to the Department of Transport in the New Year. As soon as they received it, they pressed British Rail for further information about the St Pancras option. They soon satisfied themselves that it was strongly preferable and decided to announce that and to ask Union Railways to make a detailed study and report to enable them to confirm their choice. In growing desperation, British Rail continued to press Lord Whitelaw through February and into March to ask for the Third Reading debate on the Low Level Station without admitting to him that the Government was now asking about the St Pancras option. By now wary, he stalled, and towards the end he told Lord Henderson that he was being "positively negative" to British Rail about their repeated requests.

On 16 March 1993, the Chancellor of the Exchequer included in his Budget Statement a brief announcement about the CTRL. He said that the Government now favoured the St Pancras alternative for the station and had instructed British Rail to work up a plan for a final decision.[32] On 22nd March, the Secretary of State for Transport, now John MacGregor, made a fuller statement on the CTRL[33] and Lord Caithness repeated it in the Lords.[34] Lord Henderson attended the Lords debate and pointed out to Lord Caithness that the announcement about St Pancras must mean that the King's Cross Railways Bill was now "a dead duck". With a hint of Monty Python, he asked politely, "May we please have the Minister's authority to assume that the King's Cross Railways Bill is dead?" The bill was British Rail's of course, not the Government's, so Lord Caithness replied simply, "That is a question for the promoters."

We had then to wait another ten months for Union Railways' further report on St Pancras and the Government's final decision. Union Railways established that the St Pancras scheme was fully practicable and would save £400 million against the Low Level Station, and on 24 January 1994 Mr MacGregor announced to the Commons that St Pancras had been chosen as the terminal and British Rail had been instructed to withdraw the King's Cross Railways Bill.[35]

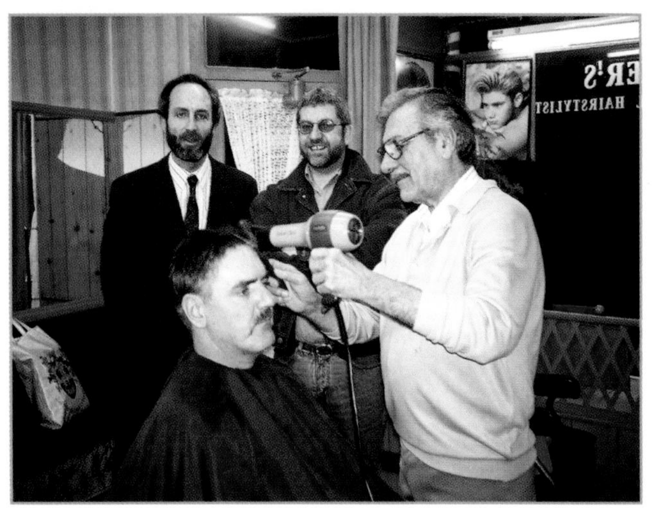

Top: Gordon Arnot and Randal Keynes tearing up the King's Cross Railways Bill outside Parliament.
Bottom: Aron Cronin and Gordon Arnot with Peter the barber sharing the news about the bill in Peter's barbershop.

Top: Randal Keynes, Margaret the florist, Freddy Groves the optician, Gordon Arnot, Derek Stuckey the landlord and Pat McMahon the publican in Margaret's shop celebrating the withdrawal of the bill.
Bottom: Gordon Arnot sharing the news about the Bill with Leo Giordani of K.C. Continental Stores.

That January day Gordon Arnot and I went to Parliament with a copy of the bill and a pocket camera. Standing on the pavement outside, we asked a slightly baffled tourist to take a photo of us tearing up the bill. We were both deeply relieved over the final withdrawal of the bill but sickened by the damage that British Rail had inflicted on South Cally during the five and a half years we'd had to fight for it. We then went back to the florist's shop in our parade to join all our friends with a bottle of champagne. Our old streets and buildings had survived the blight and decay, and now at last they could have a future again, as well as their past.

---

[1] Commons Committee report on King's Cross Railways Bill, 26 June 1990, para 28: 'It was made clear to us in evidence ...', SCCA papers, Islington Local History Centre, Finsbury Library, Islington Council.

[2] Shortly afterwards, the name was changed to King's Cross Railway Lands Group (KXRLG). KXRLG website - http://www.kxrlg.org.uk/history/timeline.pdf

[3] British Rail Information booklet 'King's Cross & St Pancras', British Rail, January 1988, SCCA papers, Islington Local History Centre, Finsbury Library, Islington Council.

[4] British Rail Environmental Statement for the King's Cross Railways Bill, SCCA papers, Islington Local Studies Centre, Finsbury Library, Islington Council.

[5] Charles Dickens, *Dombey and Son*, Penguin, 1982, Chapter 6, pp. 120-121.

[6] Alan Jackson, *London's termini,* 1985, Chapters 11, 15.

[7] 'Threat to shops in King's Cross', 14 November 1987, SCCA papers, Islington Local History Centre, Finsbury Library, Islington Council.

[8] SCCA papers, Islington Local History Centre, Finsbury Library, Islington Council.

[9] House of Commons Minutes of Proceedings, February 1988, SCCA papers, Islington Local History Centre, Finsbury Library, Islington Council.

[10] Commons Hansard, 8 May 1989, cols. 614-82 http://hansard.millbanksystems.com/commons/1989/may/08/kings-cross-railways-bill-by-order

[11] House of Commons Minutes of Evidence taken before the Committee on the King's Cross Railways Bill, 1989-1990, HC/CL/PB/2/149/4, 150/1-3. Parliamentary Archives, Houses of Parliament.

[12] Special report from Commons Committee, para 71, SCCA papers, Islington Local History Centre, Finsbury Library, Islington Council.

[13] Commons Hansard, 14 June 1990, cols. 482-4.

[14] House of Commons Session 1989-90. Special Report from the Committee on the King's Cross Railways Bill, 26 June 1990, SCCA papers, Islington Local History Centre, Finsbury Library, Islington Council.

[15] 'King's Cross scheme gets green light', David Hencke, Westminster Correspondent, *The Guardian,* 11 July 1990.

[16] Commons Hansard, 14 October 1991, cols 24-39.

[17] 'Vice gang filled our home with call-girls', *The People* 4 February 1990. Later, *The Guardian* published a feature about drugs and prostitution in King's Cross – 'King's Cross: The end of the line?', *The Guardian* Weekend Supplement 17 October 1992,

[18] Letter to Minister of State for Transport, 9 December 1991, reply from S J Lambert, 20 January 1992, SCCA papers, Islington Local History Centre, Finsbury Library, Islington Council.

[19] Commons Hansard 29 January 1992, cols 899-915.

[20] 'Channel Rail Link cut to two tracks', Daniel John, Transport Correspondent, *The Guardian* 22 May1992, and previous reports.

[21] 'King's Cross project – costs and financial viability, May 1992', SCCA papers, Islington Local History Centre, Finsbury Library, Islington Council.

[22] Michael Dynes, Transport Correspondent, *The Times* 15 May 1992.

[23] Letter from S A Robson, 20 May 1992, SCCA papers, Islington Local History Centre, Finsbury Library, Islington Council.

[24] Lords Hansard June 1992 cols 755-812.

[25] *The Guardian* obituary, 3 February 2000 - http://www.guardian.co.uk/news/2000/feb/03/guardianobituaries1

[26] House of Lords Minutes of evidence taken before the Committee on the King's Cross Railways Bill, 1992, HL/PO/PB/8/297, 300, Parliamentary Archives, Houses of Parliament.

[27] House of Lords Session 1992-93, Special Report from the Select Committee on the King's Cross Railways Bill, 16 July 1992, SCCA papers, Islington Local History Centre, Finsbury Library, Islington Council.

[28] Jack Simmons, *St Pancras Station*, 2003, Chapter 7 'St Pancras revived' by Robert Thorne pp.165ff.

[29] SCCA papers, Randal Keynes.

[30] Commons Hansard November 1992 cols. 993-1016. Details of spending provision for British Rail projects in printed statement released later.
http://hansard.millbanksystems.com/commons/1992/nov/12/autumn-statement

[31] 'BR rejects Channel Tunnel rail route', Christian Wolmar, Transport Correspondent, *The Independent* 23 December 1992.

[32] Commons Hansard 16 March 1993 cols 194-5.

[33] Commons Hansard 22 March 1993 cols 609-626.

[34] Lords Hansard 22 March 1993 cols 28-40. http://hansard.millbanksystems.com/lords/1993/mar/22/channel-tunnel-rail-link

[35] Commons Hansard 24 January 1994 cols 19-35. http://hansard.millbanksystems.com/commons/1994/jan/24/channel-tunnel-rail-link

Appendix 1

Reviving South Cally – 1994 to 2000

After the withdrawal of the King's Cross Railways Bill, plans, permission and funding for a final CTRL project took many more years to settle and our neighbours further up Caledonian Road had a long hard fight with Union Railways to protect their lives and livelihoods from severe disruption by the building works. Yet again, the railway planners ignored the effects their operations would have on people living and working in the area. Activists there campaigned for fourteen years to protect their neighbourhood from the negative impacts of the CTRL — not the Link itself, which they hoped would bring regeneration — and were largely successful.

For South Cally in 1994, although important buildings including many from the neighbourhood's industrial past, had survived, because of the seven years of British Rail's blight the neighbourhood was in the worst shape it had ever been in, with empty buildings, decayed premises and businesses failing everywhere. Even our local sex sauna had decided to sell up.

Help was at hand. Islington and Camden Council's King's Cross Regeneration Partnership made a bid for Single Regeneration funding in September 1994. Their application referred to effects that 'successive recessions, collapse of the office property market and long-term structural decline of London's economy' had had on a neighbourhood dominated by three stations and the problems they brought. They stated that 'King's Cross has a robust and diverse population whose communities have demonstrated over many years their strong commitment to the area. ...We must ensure that when investment comes it will bring benefit to, rather than alienate, the local communities of King's Cross'. This showed commitment to the area and the bid was successful. In 1997 the King's Cross Partnership agreed a Strategic Framework and funding for a range of community projects. Islington and Camden Councils concentrated on pressing needs for community services and facilities, rather than those for development. In 1995 the Thornhill Neighbourhood Project, with activists from the Copenhagen Neighbourhood Forum, helped revive the plan to open a local health centre, and in 1997 Rupert Perry, then Mayor of Islington, opened the new building in Killick Street. (See page xxx.) Alec Forshaw, Islington's Conservation Officer, recounts on the next page how Islington Council brought in many improvements in the area, for both houses and shops.

In July 1998, once the original 1983 outline planning permission had expired[1] Islington Council drew up a more detailed Planning Brief for the three street blocks immediately to the east of King's Cross Station. (See diagram on page 81) Their reason for doing this was based upon the success of the regeneration bid and also because Charlwood Alliance Holdings Ltd., a wholly owned subsidiary of P&O Property Holdings Ltd, which owned the majority of the land within these three blocks, renewed their development interest. One of the aims of this brief states that they 'help P&O and other owners to bring forward appropriate development proposals for all or any part of their landholdings by providing a local planning framework for all three street blocks'.

Finally South Cally began to flourish once the nearby blocks forming the Regent Quarter were developed. The story of this is told in the next chapter.

---

[1] In 1983, Islington Council granted outline planning permission to Stock Conversion for the redevelopment of parts of the Bravington's and Albion's Yard blocks. In the mid eighties this was acquired by P&O. This permission was due to lapse in November 1998, hence Islington's decision to produce a Planning Brief in July 1998 for Bravington's, Albion Yard and Railway Blocks, London N1.

Some of the properties improved as a result of the Conservation Area Partnership Scheme.
Photos: Mike Bruce

Appendix 2

Conservation Area Partnership Scheme

by Alec Forshaw and Mike Bruce

I became Conservation Officer for Islington in June 1988. Before then, and for many years, both Mike Bruce and I had been colleagues in the Local Plans team in Islington Planning Department, and Mike had been working tremendously hard on King's Cross. I was keen to set up a conservation team, and Mike became my deputy.

Conservation Area Partnership Schemes (CAPS) were a new English Heritage initiative in the late 1980s, promoting grants to private owners to improve historic properties in run-down commercial conservation areas. Islington was one of the first London Boroughs to take on a CAPS, which involved 50% funding from English Heritage and 50% from the Borough, and the Keystone Crescent Conservation Area was our first scheme. This included Caledonian Road south of the canal, Northdown Street, Wharfdale Road, Balfe Street and Keystone Crescent. We offered grants of between 50% and 90% to owners to improve their properties including new and repaired traditional shop fronts, cleaning, repairing and reinstating missing features on front elevations, repairing roofs and encouraging re-use of vacant upper floors.

Mike did all the leg work, a huge and sustained effort of contacting owners, leaseholders, tenants etc., obtaining and agreeing schemes and quotes from approved conservation architects (such as Tony Rees) and their contractors, completing the legal agreements with the owners, ensuring the work was done properly, making the grant payments, and subsequently monitoring that the improvement works were maintained.

The initial CAPS was for three years, but it eventually ran for twelve years. Scores of properties were improved.

We were keen to involve other partners. The Single Regeneration Budget (SRB) put in considerable funds for public realm improvements – new

York stone pavements throughout, re-laying a granite sett carriageway in Keystone Crescent (replacing the worn-out tarmac), new street lighting and CCTV, both particularly important for tackling the crime and prostitution which were then rife in the area. Housing associations became involved with the creation of flats on upper floors.

The CAPS started the process of transforming the Islington side of King's Cross. It required vision, patience and determination, and Mike had this in abundance. He did sterling work which deserves all the recognition it can get.

The physical improvements too were there for all to see, and in my opinion greatly influenced the decision of P&O (see Chapter 3) and later Peter Millican at King's Place (see Chapter 6) to take the plunge with their own investments.

The success of the King's Cross CAPS also encouraged the Council to start similar schemes elsewhere in the Borough which resulted in conservation-led regeneration in Chapel Market, Archway, Whitecross Street and Holloway Road.

The planning brief

Despite the best endeavours of the Greater London Council and various cross-boundary committees and working parties, Camden and Islington Councils never worked together as closely on King's Cross as they might have. Perhaps this isn't surprising, given that their problems and physical fabric were very different, not to mention their political priorities and community pressures. Nearly all the railway lands, gasholders etc were on the Camden side. Islington's historic fabric, both the industrial/warehouse buildings and the 1840s terraced housing, had pre-railway origins, deriving from the Regent's Canal and the Battlebridge Basin. York Way was a natural boundary. Islington had its own problems and threats and got on with solving them.

There was a degree of collaboration between 1987 and the early 1990s. In 1989 the King's Cross Conservation Areas Advisory Committee was set up by Michael Hunter with Bruce Methven of Camden Council providing administrative support. It included various local activists, including Randal Keynes from Keystone Crescent (representing SCCA) and also Malcolm Tucker representing GLIAS. The KCAAC petitioned against the King's Cross Railways Bill, making the case for both the railway lands in Camden and the buildings affected on the Islington side. In 1990 the KCAAC published a nineteen page document 'Conservation Objectives for the King's Cross Railway Lands'.

On the Islington side, the preparation and approval of planning policies and a planning brief for the street blocks affected by the CTRL railway proposals was crucial in the fight against the proposals themselves.

I was keen that the planning brief should be very specific about listing and justifying individual buildings we wanted to see retained. The other critical 'vision' of the planning brief was the idea of public pedestrian routes through and across the sites (Blocks B, C and D), where apart from the existing roads there had been none before, only dead-end alleys and yards. It also strongly promoted the idea of mixed use, affordable housing and lively ground floor uses etc.

The planning brief was finally approved by Islington's Planning Committee in October 1989. It was vital for the Parliamentary hearing on the King's Cross Railway Bill. It was a significant factor in getting the railway proposals thrown out, and for negotiating, eventually, with P&O[1].

---

[1] A later Islington planning brief, approved in 1998, incorporated, revised and extended the 1989 planning brief. It was published in July 1998, entitled *King's Cross: Bravington's, Albion Yard and Railway Blocks, London, N1 – Planning Brief, July 1998*

Top: Leo Giordani's shop, K. C. Continental Stores and Peter & Tony Barbershop, Caledonian Road, corner of Keystone Crescent, 2010.
Bottom: Tony of Peter & Tony Barbershop, 2010. This shop ceased trading in December 2011.
Photos: Angela Inglis

Top: Leo Giordani in K. C. Continental Stores, 2010.
Bottom: Leo's son, Massimo Giordani, left and customer in the delecatessen, 2010.
Photos: Angela Inglis

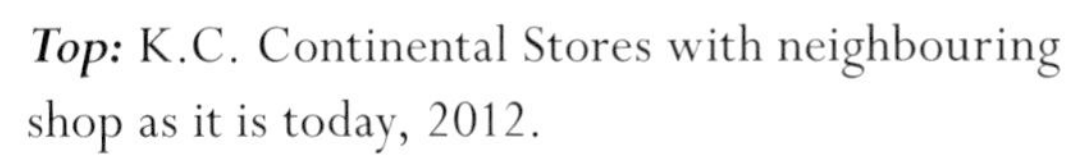

Top: K.C. Continental Stores with neighbouring shop as it is today, 2012.
Bottom: Drink Shop and Do, Caledonian Road, 2012.
Photos: Angela Inglis

Above: Kristie Bishop, Director of Drink, Shop and Do (fellow director Coralie Sleap), 2011. This shop occupies the premises of a former turkish baths, mentioned on page 151.
Photo: Angela Inglis

Above: Albert Beale, outside Housemans bookshop, Caledonian Road, 2011. Albert is director of Housemans Peace Resource Project, one of the trustees of Housemans building and on the board of the bookshop. Housemans has been at this location for over 50 years.
Photo: Angela Inglis

Top: Keystone Crescent, 2012.
Bottom: Keystone Crescent, 2012.
Photos: Angela Inglis

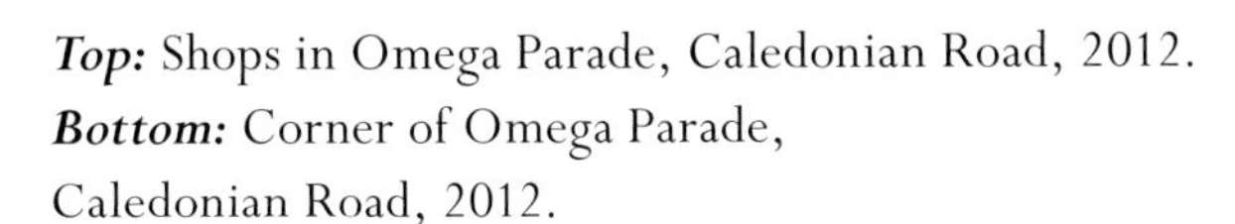

Top: Shops in Omega Parade, Caledonian Road, 2012.
Bottom: Corner of Omega Parade,
Caledonian Road, 2012.
Photos: Angela Inglis

Above: Some of the Stuckey family at Keystone Crescent, 2010. Clockwise, top left, Nadia, Bob, Dmitri and Liz.
Photo: Angela Inglis

The 'Lighthouse', corner of Gray's Inn Road and Pentonville Road.

Corner of Caledonian Road and Pentonville Road.

The Scala, Corner of Pentonville Road and King's Cross Bridge.

Note: The buildings illustrated here would have been destroyed if the international station had been built at King's Cross.

Chapter 3

Regent Quarter

The restoration of the Regent Quarter

by Angela Inglis

Introduction

The Regent Quarter consists of three blocks bordered to the east by Balfe Street and Caledonian Road, to the west by York Way, to the south by Pentonville Road and to the north by Wharfdale Road. The area was so named by P&O Properties Ltd who acquired much of it in the mid 1980s. This chapter is about the Regent Quarter's redevelopment and reinvigoration.

During the 1970s and 80s Islington Council had opposed suggestions from local residents that the whole area be designated a conservation area, considering the industrial buildings to have insufficient architectural quality and the area to lack cohesion.1

However in 1978 Islington's Planning Department undertook a local listing survey that included several of the area's distinctive industrial buildings. In 1986, the Greater London Council's Historic Buildings Divisiondesignated the King's Cross Conservation Area, which straddled Camden and Islington and included the three blocks covered here. Islington had previously designated the Keystone Conservation Area for the residential terraces further east.2

Meanwhile, other planning decisions had been playing a part in the dereliction of the area. In 1983, Islington Council had granted outline planning permission, valid for fifteen years, to Stock Conversion for the redevelopment of parts of the Bravington's and Albion Yard blocks

An artist's representation of how the Regent Quarter conservation area could look. The image places the scheme in context within the broader King's Cross area, showing King's Cross station immediately to the west. *Image: Courtesy P&O*

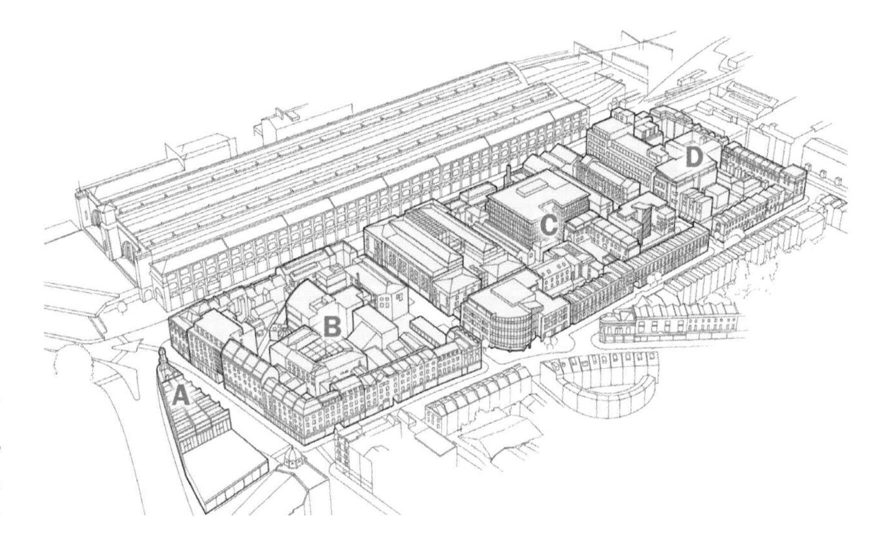

The Regent Quarter regeneration area, in blue, showing the block names.
Image: Courtesy RHWL

(for office space, squash courts, a restaurant and shop). Shortly afterwards Stock Conversion sold the land with this outline planning permission to P&O.

In 1989 Islington's Planning Committee drew up a Planning Brief for the three blocks, identifying buildings which it would be desirable to keep. It strongly stipulated mixed use including residential - not a monoculture of large office blocks. Conservation Officers Alec Forshaw and Mike Bruce were closely involved in the brief. This was revised in greater detail in a comprehensive Planning Brief from Islington Council published in 1998, to coincide with the lapsing of the 1983 outline planning permission. The 1998 document was ahead of its time in its sensitive approach to the area.

Regent Quarter

2000 and after

At the end of February 2000, P&O submitted planning applications through their subsidiary Charlwood Alliance Holdings Ltd for the mixed rebuilding and adaptation of their properties for residential, retail and office accommodation.3 They named the Blocks B, C and D, from south to north, Block A was their name for the 'Lighthouse' block, south of Pentonville Road and under Camden Council's jurisdiction (see photo on page 76). The applications went to public consultation in June and various revisions were submitted in October 2000.

One of the objectors was Malcolm Tucker[4] of the Greater London Industrial Archaeology Society (GLIAS). He and some of his colleagues had taken a particular interest in the distinctive industrial buildings of the site for several years and had collaborated with the Royal Commission on the Historic Monuments of England (RCHME) in surveying some of them in 1996. On 22nd June 2000, eight months before P&O's plans went before the Islington Planning Committee for approval, Malcolm wrote to the planners on behalf of GLIAS:

> 'We write in objection to the demolition of certain buildings in the Albion Yard block. The area immediately east of King's Cross Station, centred on Albion Yard, is one of the few remaining blocks in north London with a coherent nineteenth century industrial character.'

Malcolm noted the architecture and historic uses of many buildings, including a copper and brass works of circa 1866, a late 19th century commercial warehouse, an emery paper works and an ironworks warehouse dated 1866.

> 'The York Way frontages are... scarce examples of the metropolitan industrial architecture of the period... Some of the few such buildings in London that are visible from a major thoroughfare.'

Initially, according to Alec Forshaw,[5] 'English Heritage had been cautious about getting heavily involved with the P&O sites. This was partly because Islington Council had been working on plans for the area for a very long time, and partly because English Heritage's remit was advisory rather than one of direction. At the time of the initial application only one of the buildings on the Islington P&O sites was statutorily listed, No. 7 Caledonian Road, (see photo on page 111). The so-called Lighthouse Building, Block A, within the London Borough of Camden had been listed in 1997 but was not part of the application. The Islington side did not involve the demolition of any statutorily listed buildings, only ones locally listed by Islington. English Heritage expected Islington to take the lead, and did not appear to want to stand in the way of P&O's initial scheme.

'Nevertheless English Heritage were very aware of what was going on, largely because of the excellent relationship between myself at Islington and Paddy Pugh, the case officer in English Heritage whose patch included Islington. Somewhat controversially at the time, English Heritage decided to raise the public awareness of this part of King's Cross by holding the launch of their new 'Power of Place' policy document on the P&O site.

'With P&O's permission the launch was held at 8.30 am on Thursday 14th December 2000 in the then disused ground floor of the St Pancras Ironworks building behind 40 York Way. Some of the objectors to the P&O scheme took this to be a sign that English Heritage implicitly supported P&O's current proposals. There was some confusion about who was invited to attend and who wasn't, but a small and polite protest in the courtyard outside the Ironworks, led by Lisa Pontecorvo,[6] was sensitively defused when Neil Cossons, Chairman of English Heritage, invited everyone inside for breakfast. However, according to Andrew Bosi who was present, Lisa, on principle, "declined to eat".

Lisa Pontecorvo persuaded Jeannie Burnett, as the chair of the Islington Conservation Advisory Committee, into getting involved with the Regent Quarter. Jeannie Burnett wrote to the Chair of Islington Planning Committee on 2nd February 2001[7]

> 'You are probably aware that the P&O planning application for the redevelopment at King's Cross is coming before the Planning Committee on 20th February 2001. In my opinion the scheme remains fundamentally flawed for the following main reasons:
>
> The huge new tourist hotel and office block will be monolithic which will result in very dead streets at evenings and weekends

and for this reason the environment and personal safety are of huge concern.

There should be far more residential use on upper floors in all the street blocks and a decent amount of affordable housing generally.

A greater variety of land uses, including shops, restaurants, bars, studios, offices, should be provided at ground floor level, to bring life to the area.

The new buildings are too big and too bland. There is virtually nothing in the scheme for the local community.

The retention and re-use of more of the interesting existing buildings would help in all of the above.

It is the intention of P&O to demolish existing buildings and clear the sites without any commitment to a contract for new buildings.

I hope you will do all you can to ensure that this disastrous proposal is rejected.'

Jeannie Burnett, on behalf of the Islington King's Cross Conservation Area Advisory Sub-Committee[8].

Earlier, Lucinda Lambton told Jeannie Burnett[9] she was doing a programme on industrial buildings. Did Jeannie have any suggestions? Jeannie said, "Do I?" and introduced her to the Conservation Advisory Committee. Lucinda Lambton then made a BBC radio programme entitled "Bringing Down the House" about the P&O Blocks which was broadcast in November 2000.[10] On 2nd February, 2001[11] she wrote to Dr Bridget Cherry, Editor of The Buildings of England and an English Heritage Commissioner.

'I am writing to plead for the saving of the Pontifex Brass Foundry at King's Cross, the positively surreal survival of an intact 19th century factory, that still, unbelievably, is standing in the middle of London; a warren of 19th century industrial life; of cobbled alleys; of a [staircase with each] riser of each step smothered in fanciful design... as well as an ornate crane still hanging proud on the wall. Although these are the elements, which individually are somewhat unremarkable, by their survival together, they have become most remarkable – an excellent example of how, after a hundred or so years, the ordinary becomes rare.

That such a survival as this should be demolished in favour of a car park is terrifying. Surely by now we have all too miserably learnt the error of such short-sighted destruction of such historic sights!'

Before the Planning Meeting scheduled for 20th February 2001, Jeannie Burnett marshalled committed and impressive speakers to be there.[12] Meanwhile, the team in the Islington Council office was also making preparations, as Alec Forshaw explains:[13]

'P&O's starting position was that they needed a large hotel and a large office block in Block C in order to kick-start any development in the area. At that time there were still ownership problems with Block B, particularly the joinery works in Caledonia Street which P&O didn't own.

'P&O's initial proposals involved the demolition of most of Block C, including Pontifex and most of Albion Yard. The Islington Director of Development at the time (and throughout the whole period of the negotiations) was Ian Crawley. He was sympathetic on the basis that 'something was better than nothing.' While it might be unfair to suggest that he was keen to get something built while he was still at Islington, he did say that he wanted to give P&O their own way because something had to happen at King's Cross after so long. The P&O proposals, of course, ran contrary to much in the Planning Brief.

‘In the office Mike Bruce and I had drawn up a large scale plan of Block C showing how a new hotel and office block could be built whilst also retaining the historic buildings identified in the Planning Brief.

‘Ian Crawley was insistent on a unified corporate view from the Planning Department, and while he was very aware of Mike’s and my strong opposition to P&O’s scheme, he did not want this to be expressed outside the office. Nevertheless, I decided that the ideas should be shared with the Conservation Advisory Panel, who had looked at and criticised P&O’s original proposals.

‘Part of my job was to run the Conservation Advisory Committee Design Panel on which all the national, borough and local amenity societies were represented. They were already well aware of the P&O proposals and there was a growing campaign of objection from many sources.

‘The proposals, on the instruction of Ian Crawley, were recommended for approval by the planning case officer at the Planning Committee in February 2001. Before the meeting Ian advised me that I should not attend. When I said that it was a public meeting and he couldn’t stop me, he said that if I did attend, then on no account was I allowed to speak.

‘The meeting was in the Council Chamber, and packed with people filling all the seats in the public gallery. I sat near the front to one side, but visible to the Committee members. After the presentation by the planning officer of the scheme, with its recommendations for approval, Councillor Rupert Perry turned to me and said, “I see that the Council’s Conservation Officer is here, and I’d like to hear what he has to say”. So, I said my bit, that there was disagreement within the Planning Department, and that I thought there was an alternative and better way which could retain many of the historic buildings. The floor was then opened up to the objectors, many of whom spoke with tremendous power and authority.'

The following account of the meeting is drawn from an article by Diana Shelley, in *Network*, the King's Cross Railway Lands Group's magazine.[14]

'A late letter from English Heritage was read to the meeting underlining many of the points speakers had made. As well as challenging plans to destroy buildings such as the Pontifex works on Albion Yard, it criticised P&O's failure to develop a master plan for all four blocks (including the 'lighthouse' block on Pentonville Road in Camden and 'Block D' between Railway Street and Wharfdale Road). It would, English Heritage said, be premature to grant the application before these issues were resolved.'

Randal Keynes, a former King's Cross Railway Lands Group activist, representing the Victorian Society, lambasted the designs which would overshadow 'one of the great railway stations in the world'. It was, he said, 'a casual, careless, heartless commercial redevelopment'.

'Terence Kelly, chair of the Copenhagen Forum planning sub-committee and a local resident, denounced the scheme as a wasted opportunity to redevelop the area to a high standard.

'Local resident John Ashwell reported that residents on Wharfdale Road wanted the scheme to go ahead, if only to get a new traffic scheme. But Ian Lerner,[15] of Islington's Conservation Advisory Committee, contended that after thirty years of decay a proper mixed use scheme was essential.

'Former King's Cross Railwayland's Group chair, Andrew Bosi, speaking for the Islington Society, pointed out the threat to local democracy. The plan was essentially only an outline and if the committee agreed it they would have little control over detailed plans.

> ‘Rupert Perry, councillor for Thornhill Ward where the development would take place, said “We’ve waited a long time, we’re still waiting, and we’re happy to wait a little longer for a better scheme.’

Several members of the committee spoke against the scheme including Councillor Jenny Sands. She made a point by point criticism of the lack of strategic thinking. She stressed that having so few homes contradicted the Government’s policies on ‘planning out crime.’

An unexpected speaker was Councillor Brian Woodrow, Camden chair of planning, who said his committee had not yet taken a view. On that basis, Islington decided to defer their decision till they heard from Camden.

Objectors were disappointed that the application was merely deferred rather than rejected outright. However the planning officers then told P&O to come back with a new, detailed master plan, to include 200 homes.

Plans revised

P&O, led by Director Gary Brooks, assisted by Graham Corser, his fellow director, did indeed revise their plans for the Regent Quarter. While Islington’s planning committee merely deferred their decision, P&O grasped the nettle and decided to start again, with new architects.

At long last they consulted local people before redeveloping the plans too far. They discussed outline ideas in several small meetings, including local residents, members of the Copenhagen Neighbourhood Forum and Islington’s Conservation Advisory Committee.

While there were still problems, not least how best to manage traffic around the site, there were some visible gains. Block D (from Wharfdale Road down to Railway Street) was now included as part of the worked up scheme, and there was to be some housing within Block B, the Bravington block from Caledonia Street to Pentonville Road. P&O hoped to re-submit a full planning application by the autumn of 2001. No doubt there would still be parts of their plans that local people disagreed with (and local people could object as part of normal planning procedures). But they had made a start at listening to local concerns as well as giving hope for real regeneration on the site.

When Diana Shelley interviewed Gary Brooks for the King's Cross Voices oral history project in 2007[16] she asked whether he was involved in drawing up the first application for the Regent Quarter. He said,

> "Not personally, I was very much on the periphery and was still working on other developments with P& O at the time, and it was shortly after the first scheme was deferred that I physically got very involved, and as part of that we changed architects. We thought we needed to have a fresh view. New pairs of eyes as it were. We had been working on the scheme for three or four years before then, not really seriously enough. I and my fellow director brought in new architects, one of whom was Peter Shaw from RHWL[17] and another Richard Griffiths.[18] They brought some fresh ideas and I realised we had been a little bit too ivory towerish in our approach, that we should go and talk to a lot more of the local people and local groups, which for the next six months we did. The discussions ranged from people who were very angry with us because we were doing things they didn't want us to do to people saying you will never build it, to people saying you just want to make a lot of money. I pointed out that as developers, if we didn't make money we didn't build buildings and that there was a viability issue behind every scheme."

This change in attitude by P&O, led by Gary Brooks, impressed everyone involved in the campaign to save the Regent Quarter. As Diana Shelley says in the interview with him, 'Not many developers get a bit of a set-back who immediately come back and say "Okay, what do you want?" Gary Brooks replied that they wanted to come up with a scheme that worked both for the community and for P&O and its shareholders. There were long negotiations about keeping some buildings, putting certain things in like the supermarket which the locals wanted, and being very truthful with people. Gary Brooks thought that beforehand, maybe, because there hadn't been enough consultation, there was a lot of distrust, and so they

Alec Forshaw (left) and Mike Bruce in Albion Walk, Block C.
Photo: Angela Inglis

went out and said to people, "This is what we want to do, we need to make money, otherwise we can't do it...we will clean up King's Cross."

Revised scheme[19]

The significantly amended scheme went out to public consultation in August 2001, and was approved by the Planning Committee on 4th December. Gary Brooks says in his interview that when, "towards the end of 2001 we went back to another planning committee with the revised scheme, after we had spent six months talking to people, we had a dozen people stand up and say why the committee ought to vote in favour of P&O, which was very pleasing and a good night for us." Consent was finally granted, with conditions, in June 2002.

Alec Forshaw remembers[20]

'When Islington's Planning Committee did the correct thing in February 2001, English Heritage became more actively involved. Following the ideas initially sketched by myself and Mike Bruce, Anthony Delarue prepared a beautifully drawn alternative scheme on behalf of Islingtion Conservation Advisory Committee (see pages 128 – 131). English Heritage commissioned at their own expense Richard Griffiths Architects to work these up into a more detailed scheme. They also, crucially, commissioned an economic appraisal which showed that the figures would stack up. This was a vital bit of work in persuading P&O to change tack.

'As it happened, following pressure from Islington, the Victorian Society and others, No.34B York Way, with its wonderful timber trussed roof, was statutorily listed in August 2001, and the former stables at the rear of No.55 Balfe Street, with its horse ramps and stalls, were listed in November 2001.

'Both Rupert Perry and Councillor Jenny Sands were great allies to the cause, and both realised that something better was possible. The revised scheme for Block C was, of course, a huge improvement, but there were still compromises. The loss of Nos. 24-28 York Way, including the pub on the corner with Caledonia Street and the so-called Boot Black Brigade building at No. 28 were significant and regrettable. The demolition of the northern end of the Jahn Building, both the front and back part, in order to allow a frontage for the new office building onto York Way was also a compromise, although it has worked out quite well.

'Subsequently Mike and I had numerous battles with P&O and their architects over various details, such as the retention of the original iron windows to the Ironworks on Railway Street (which we lost), the retention of the original granite cobbles to Albion Yard (which we won).

'Some details, such as the St Pancras Ironworks external staircase at the rear of Pontifex, were reproduced rather than keeping and repairing the original.

'I would have liked to have seen more lively uses, such as a café, within Albion Yard and the little piazza behind Pontifex, rather than ground-floor residential which is rather too deadening.

'On Block B, when the whole site was eventually assembled by P&O, the critical compromise was the loss of the Bravington Building to allow a way through from Pentonville Road. We succeeded in rescuing and reclaiming the fabulous dome which had sat above the rear showroom for use elsewhere in the scheme, and we eventually persuaded P&O that the so-called Varnish Works (in fact a varnish warehouse) could make an attractive pedestrian space fronted by cafes and bars. We lost, sadly, the magnificent panelled ground floor of the Nat West Bank on Pentonville Road (now the bookmakers). P&O were adamant that no occupier would want it. Of course, it would have made the most fabulous restaurant'

'We did, however, retain the old 'refreshments' sign, painted on the brickwork at the southern end of York Way and it is excellent that Block D is now on site.'

Changes for the better

The campaigners were adamant that it was important to have a mixed development and that some of the offices should be turned into flats. Their point was proved when 20 of the 100 apartments sold out in the first weekend.[21] It was the offices that were hard to let as there had been a downturn in the market.

Gary Brooks, on behalf of P&O, receives the Islington Society Award for Best Architecture in 2006 from Lord Chris Smith. *Photo: Supplied by Gary Brooks*

Gary Brooks says in his 2007 interview,

> "The biggest change we made was to keep some of the buildings that seemed more important to local people and to put more residential into the scheme. We were very clear that internal surveillance from people who own homes is much better than surveillance by the police, or from other bodies. The flats are all let. It's a very pleasant place to be and you wouldn't know you were next to a major transportation hub when you are inside the blocks. In design terms it's something that no one could have foreseen, how tranquil it can be inside those blocks. I think one of the other elements that has been fantastically pleasing is the way the external hard landscaping has worked inside the blocks where we have re-used some of the artefacts that have been associated with the previous uses of the buildings, the industrial uses and the way we have incorporated artwork into King's Cross."

Diana Shelley writing in *Network* in the summer of 2004, on the first phase of the development, commented, 'Which buildings could be saved was always contentious. After decades of neglect, they were in poor condition but most have been kept and, from what I saw, rehabilitated with care and sensitivity. Mixed among them are good, modern buildings which keep to a proper scale and respect their nineteenth century context – I think the mix works well.'

Gary Brooks said in 2007[22]

> 'I have a great affection for what P&O have done down at King's Cross, it has come out better than anybody thought it possibly could do, particularly the way the new buildings interact with the old. It is a great exemplar of how the new and the old can fit together and how commercialism and conservation can sit side by side.' In 2006 P&O were presented with the Islington Society Award for Best Architecture that year.[23]

Regent Quarter is a rare example where a community's successful opposition to an inappropriate development led to a creative collaboration between developers and local people, which has worked for both. Other developers could learn from its success.

---

[1] Information from Alec Forshaw, Islington Conservation Officer, 1988 to 2007 'Following the Civic Amenities Act 1967 the London Borough of Islington designated several conservation areas, including in 1970 the Keystone Crescent Conservation Area, which included Balfe Street and the early 19th century terraces to the east in Northdown Street and Caledonian Road north of Keystone Crescent. In 1981 following pressure from the London Canals Committee, the Council designated the Regent's Canal West Conservation Area which included the water of the canal and Battlebridge Basin, but very few of the buildings actually fronting the canal. During the 1970s and 1980s Islington Council had been opposed to suggestions from local residents and amenity societies that the whole area down to Pentonville Road should be designated as a conservation area. Even the Conservation Officer, Geoffrey Gribble, had been unconvinced, thinking that the industrial buildings were of insufficient architectural quality and that the area lacked cohesive quality.'

[2] Information from Alec Forshaw, February 2012. Fortunately the Greater London Council also had powers to designate conservation areas, although they rarely used them, but did so in 1986 at King's Cross, shortly before the GLC was abolished. Several members of the excellent GLC Historic Buildings Division transferred to jobs in the newly-created

English Heritage London Region. Islington Council later extended the King's Cross Conservation Area to form a contiguous area linking with Keystone Crescent and the Regent's Canal

[3] LB Islington, full planning application P000434, conservation area consent application P000433 and listed building application P000432 (the last named was for 7 Caledonian Road). These numbers were retained through to the consents finally granted on 10 th June 2002

[4] Malcolm Tucker, engineering historian and archaeologist

[5] Alec Forshaw, Islington Conservation Officer, as above

[6] Film researcher (retired) and an environmental activist in Islington

[7] Jeannie Burnett's archives

[8] Sub-Committee members:

- Anthony Delarue, Architect, Anthony Delarue Associates, London N1 1EN
- David Gibson, Architect and Chair, Islington Preservation Trust,
- Professor Philip James, Hon Professor of Nutrition, London School of Hygiene and Tropical Medicine,
- Ian Lerner, Ian Lerner & Co 10 Eagle Ct London EC1M 5QD Developer who contributed to saving Clerkenwell,
- Councillor Rupert Perry, Islington Thornhill Ward

[9] Information given to Angela Inglis by Jeannie Burnett December 2011

[10] From Lisa Pontecorvo's letter to Dr Bridget Cherry, November 19th 2000

[11] Copy of this letter in Jeannie Burnett's archives

[13] Information from TAJ Burnett

[14] Information given to Angela Inglis by Alec Forshaw December, 2011

[15] Network, Issue 35. Newsletter of King's Cross Railway Lands Development Forum, date

[16] See note [12] above, member of the Islington Conservation Area Advisory Committee

[17] King's Cross Voices Project, Interview with Gary Brooks, 16th March 2007, Interviewer Diana Shelley

[18] Renton Howard Wood Levin LLP,
Ivory House, St Katharine Docks, London E1W 1AT

[19] Richard Griffiths Architects 5 Maidstone Mews 72-76 Borough High St London SE1 1GN

[20] The scheme now included additional applicactions, P011873 and P011874

[21] Text given to Angela Inglis by Alec Forshaw, 2nd December 2011

[22] Information given to Angela Inglis by Jeannie Burnett, December 2011

[23] King's Cross Voices Interview, see note 23 above

[24] Lord Chris Smith presented the award to Gary Brooks

Albion Yard

Above: Entrance to Albion Yard from Balfe Street. Running across the far end of the yard is Albion Walk.
Below: Detail of the roof at the entrance as seen from inside the yard.

ALBION YARD

Northwest corner.
Through the arch is the
continuation of Albion Walk to Railway Street.

The Brassworks

View from York Way towards Albion Walk with The Brassworks on the left. Displayed is a rare internal glimpse of the present use as an architectural office. Refer to photo on page 144.

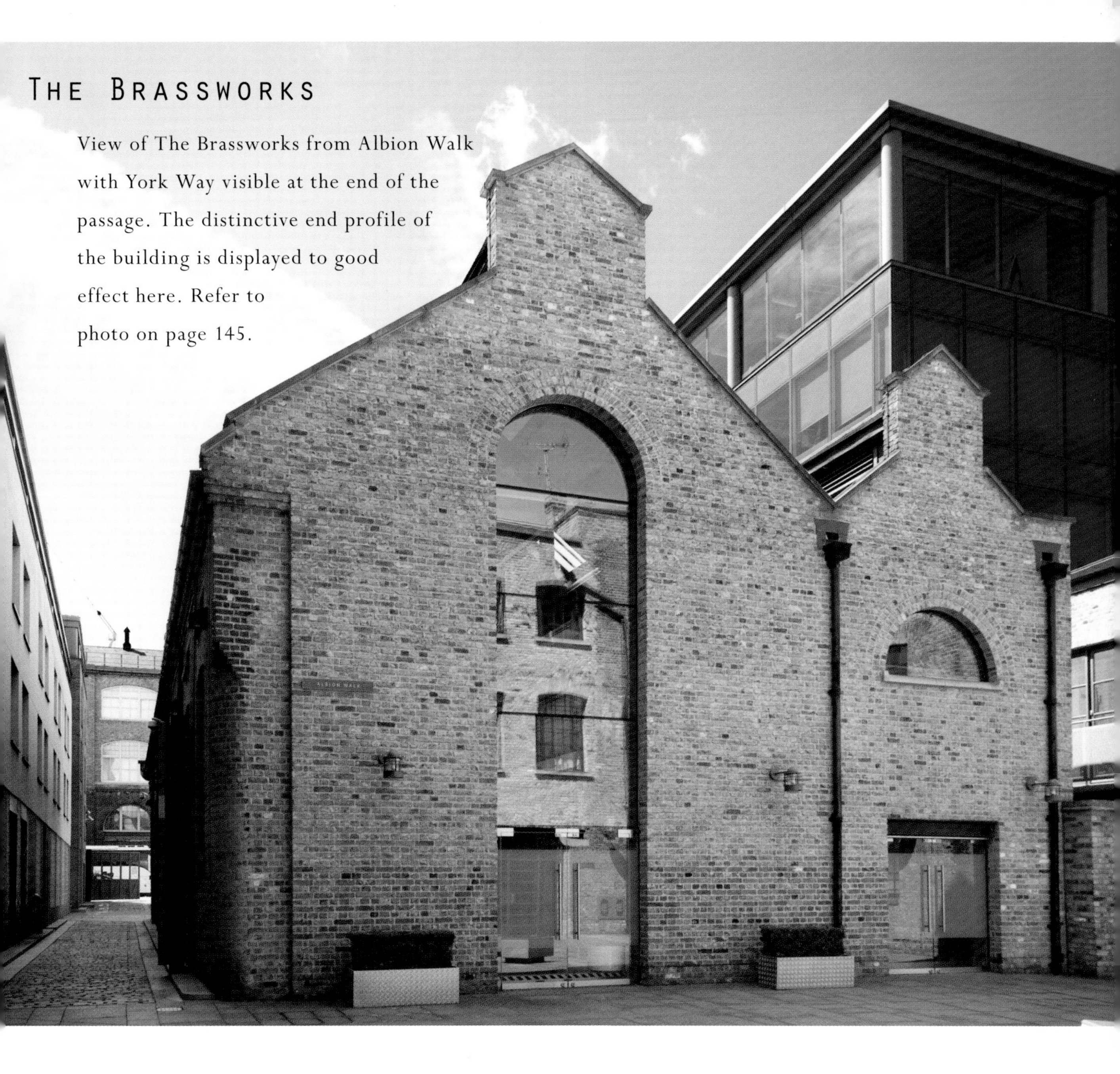

THE BRASSWORKS

View of The Brassworks from Albion Walk with York Way visible at the end of the passage. The distinctive end profile of the building is displayed to good effect here. Refer to photo on page 145.

Albion Buildings

To the right of The Brassworks in the courtyard in Albion Walk.

The passageway to the left leads to Albion Yard and Railway Street.

Albion Buildings

The courtyard opposite The Brassworks in Albion Walk. The gear mechanism by the entrance, under the stairs, was recovered from inside this building where it was once used to winch items up to the top floor. Refer to photo on page 145.

Winch Gear

Albion Buildings, Albion Walk.

Albion Walk

Leading from Albion Buildings towards Albion Yard.

ALBION YARD

Office oriel window in Albion Yard.

ALBION YARD

Block end facing oriel window. See photo, page 141.

ALBION WALK

Southern entrance to Albion Walk from Caledonia Street. The glazed roof over the entrance was relocated from the former Bravington premises at 296-298 Pentonville Road.

ALBION WALK

Looking north along Albion Walk from The Brassworks and Albion Buildings towards Albion Yard and Railway Street.

Varnisher's Yard

The passageway to Varnisher's Yard from Bravington's Walk.

The reflection in the window shows the outside area of Bar Pepito.

Varnisher's Yard

Bar Pepito, showing preserved architectural detail.

Varnisher's Yard

Opposite the entrance from Bravington's Walk is the exit to Caledonian Road. See photo, page 153.

Bravington's Walk

Adjacent to The Laundry is this fascinating combination of old and new architecture clustered around the exit to York Way.

The Laundry

The rear side of the King's Cross Laundry, as seen in Bravington's Walk, adjacent to a new glass fronted development.

CLEANING
DYEING

Varnisher's Yard

Passageway between Varnisher's Yard and the street *(left)*, and entrance from the street in Caledonian Road *(right)*.

Left: On the passage wall is an intricately decorated ceramic maze by Philip O'Reilly, 2005. ΩIt reflects the warren like nature of the Regent Quarter and contains references to the local area. This includes a tribute to Charles Dickens with a quote describing King's Cross from "Our Mutual Friend". See photos on page 152.

Right: 7, Caledonian Road, former varnish manufacturers displaying a tile-hung, Arts-and-Crafts-styled façade.

Preserved Roof Structures

Left: Trussed roof of the main Pontifex Works, now The Brassworks in Albion Walk.

Above: Hipped roof structure of The Hub, a business meetings centre.

34 York Way

Renovated buildings at 34 York Way, earlier occupied by Jahn, the machinery importers (see photo on page 144) and originally part of the Pontifex Works (see map on page 134). ***Left:*** Previously an open space now incorporated into the interior. Panels of a sectional cast-iron water tank are set into the wall at the far end. *Photo: Chris Hollick, courtesy RHWL.* ***Above:*** Heavy timber roof over a workshop built for Pontifex. *Photos: Courtesy of EC Harris.*

34-40 York Way

Renovated buildings on York Way, the western edge of Regent Quarter. The chimney stack was formerly part of a boilerhouse. Behind is the contemporary glass fronted entrance to 34 York Way. Right of this is the remaining frontage of the old Jahn machinery importers. The grey panel conceals the surviving porton of the Jahn sign. Compare this to the 1986 photo on page 144 showing the complete building. To the left of the chimney is The Hub, a business meeting centre, formerly belonging to Albion Yard. This building, prior to redevelopment, can be seen on page 144. Also, the renovated heavy timber roof structure can be seen on page 113.

THE
ALL
ENQUIRIES
37-5488
CHIPS

The Lighthouse

The "Lighthouse" block (see diagram page 81) a well known King's Cross landmark at the southern end of Regent Quarter, by the junction of Pentonville Road, Gray's Inn Road and Euston Road. It gets its name from the zinc-clad wooden structure *(above left)* at the apex of the building. The block will be renovated as a separate development.

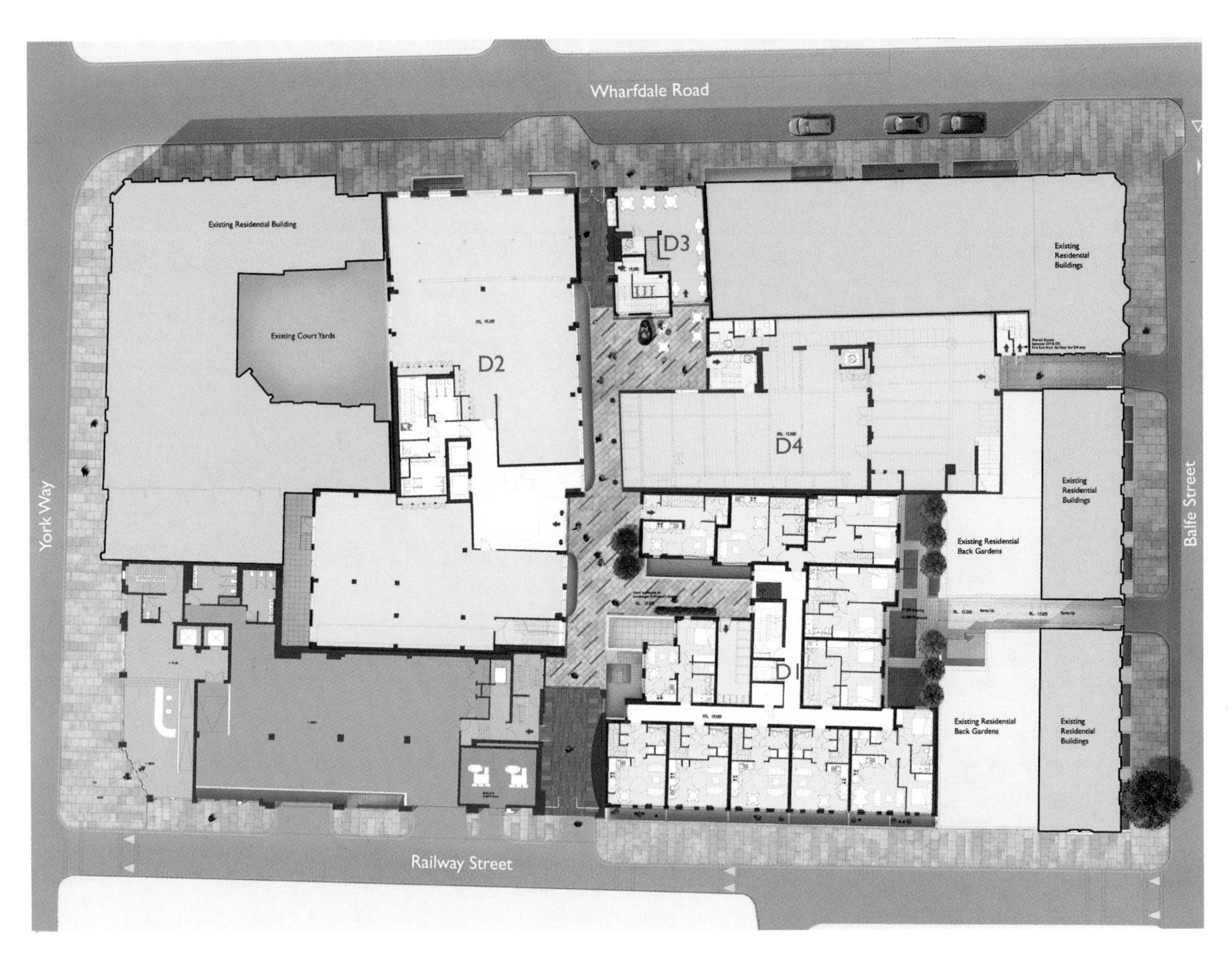

Regent Quarter block D ground floor plan.
Image: © and courtesy of RHWL

D1: 35 residential 1 and 2 bed apartments
D2: 3,309 sq. m of commercial office space
D3: 133 sq. m of cafe/restaurant space with three 2 bed apartments above
D4: 757 sq. m of commercial studio offices

An architect's overview

by Peter Shaw

I studied architecture at Cambridge in the early 1970s, and began my working career in London with Sandy Wilson's office working on the British Library. I joined RHWL at the start of the 1980s and have been there ever since, mainly carrying out large projects.

Kings Cross

Kings Cross came into my life in March 2001 with a phone call from Gary Brooks of P&O asking us to take a fresh look at a scheme which had just been deferred at the Islington Planning Committee. As I write this the end of our work is coming into sight. At a meeting of Islington's Planning Committee in October 2011 we were granted consent for 42–50 York Way, the last remaining one of over 40 buildings that have been renovated, converted or constructed on the site during the past 10 years.

Consultation

Before we started to design anything or put pen to paper we had talks with all the people who had an interest in the area. This turned out to be quite a voyage of discovery, involving well over twenty interested parties, from the residents themselves to the police, heritage groups and the planning officers and their consultees. There were to be some interesting surprises.

The area, known later as Regent Quarter, was in 2001 one of the roughest areas of prostitution and drug dealing in the capital. It had been largely derelict for twenty years or more. Our discussions with the police were serious debates about how to design out the all too visible daily crime. One of the initial design suggestions, a new pedestrian route through the middle of the site, was greeted with deep concern, as creating a hundred new quiet corners where evil could be done out of sight of the main roads. When we met local residents we polled them for their dearest wishes, expecting to see law and order top of the list. To our genuine surprise, the clear winner was the desire for a supermarket, a wish that we and P&O were more than happy to fulfil. I am pleased to record that the crime itself disappeared as soon as the contractor's hoarding went up around the site, effectively making it impossible.

Euston Road gyratory

The best surprise came from an unexpected quarter. The deferred scheme had had several faults, foremost among them was that it involved the demolition of too many buildings, especially the superb trussed and raftered factory that had been a brass foundry. The main reason for this was that a large slice was being removed from the available land to widen Caledonia Street into a northern arm of the traffic gyratory system of the Inner London Ringroad. This long standing road scheme effectively meant widening Caledonia Street to three lanes, making it one way and putting the traffic from the Euston Road through the site. At one meeting with P&O when we were wrestling with the many obstacles that appeared to be in the way of a good scheme, their chairman Bill Egerley suggested we should get rid of the damned road, and we all laughed, thinking it impossible.

Soon afterwards we had a consultation meeting with Islington Highways Department, and we asked about the gyratory road widening and how dreadful was its affect on any scheme. Yes, they said, we don't like it either but that's nothing to do with us, that's Camden's responsibility because they look after York Way. Some time later when we met Camden's Highways they said no, it wasn't them it was Transport for London because they look after the Euston Road. Later still we met TFL, and they knew nothing about it, it wasn't in their plans, it was something in the Islington local plan but they didn't need it. We realised that it belonged to nobody and was wanted by no-one and so we gleefully abandoned it. This unlocked the land jigsaw puzzle, making the retention of the Brassworks easy, removed a blight on the future environment of Regent Quarter and made many other good things possible.

New masterplan

The old buildings on the site are an interesting variety carried out by many business owners over a fair period of time in the Victorian and Edwardian era, following the arrival of the canal and railways. This is one aspect of the area that gives it its character, the relatively small scale of each building and the lack of architectural uniformity, though all within a consistent palette of materials. We were keen that the new buildings we inserted did not strike too uniform a note in this context, by looking as though they were all the work of one hand.

There were also gaps around the edges of the blocks caused by the demolition of some of the buildings on the site in the past. These we sought to fill in so that the street frontages were once more continuous.

The walkway through the site has proved to be a success, but the idea was not without its misgivings. The objective was to achieve a tranquil and varied pedestrian route along which could be cafes and restaurants giving life, and from which some of the buildings could be entered. The movement of sufficient people along it would make it self policing. However, given the prevailing background of crime, we were obliged to provide gates to it at its points of entry which to some extent raised the spectre of a gated community divorced from the city and inaccessible to the general public. So far I'm pleased to say the use of the gates has been confined to the hours of darkness.

However, with the exception of those in Block B near to the Euston Road the cafes and restaurants have not succeeded. Maybe the fact that the walkway is yet to be completed through Block D to Wharfdale Road has restricted footfall, or maybe the population is not yet enough to sustain them, but one is now converted to offices and another has been omitted from Block D for fear of it not finding a tenant. Having said that the restaurants in the small courtyard inside Block B have been a great success, perhaps due to their proximity to the station and Euston Road.

The retained buildings, once we had agreed which ones they were going to be, were in many ways the simplest in terms of design, though they proved the opposite when it came to construction, given their age and long period of neglect.

We wanted to make York Way and Caledonian Road into two-way streets again, and had work done by highways engineers that proved it to be possible. One-way streets and conservation areas are poor bedfellows, having two-way traffic causes traffic to slow down and somehow makes the cars less dominant. But in this we have, so far, failed.

The end in sight

The majority of the work was carried out between 2002-2005. The area soon came back to life and our energies were directed to the last area of dereliction, romantically known as Block D, the area between Wharfdale Road and Railway Street. Here a crucial piece of land ownership had long been missing, making it impossible to get the walkway through the site from Railway Street to Wharfdale Road without demolishing the end of the only listed building on the site, a very pleasant two storey stable building built for the London General Omnibus Co. in 1910. In 2007 P&O acquired this missing piece and we were able to bring forward a much improved plan that made for better buildings in more sensible locations, and kept the stables intact. This mixed use scheme is currently commencing construction and should be finished in 2013.

The final piece of the jigsaw, for us at least, is 42-50 York Way, the post war Book Warehouse on the corner of Railway Street and York Way which has been in temporary use as a dance studio. The proposal to convert this to offices was given consent in October 2011.

Peter Shaw
Photo: Angela Inglis

Islington Conservation Advisory Committee

by Anthony Delarue

Following the reversal at planning committee of P&O's draconian development plans, which would have swept away all the heritage buildings immediately to the east of King's Cross station, the Islington Conservation Advisory Committee (CAC) suggested that some of its architect members might give some guidance on the approach it would be happy to see.

CAC, which had been one of the leading lights of the public campaign against the proposals during the consultation stage, took the unusual step of arguing that the only workable way forward was for P&O to change architects, to appoint a firm with a more conservation-based approach. This was argued forcibly at an early meeting with the developers.

The CAC argument was that by integrating the development into the fabric of the existing townscape, and building upon the significant amount of early industrial heritage (the ironworks, Jahn building, the Pontifex foundry, the black lead and washing blue works) the developer would benefit from a higher-quality development, leading to higher returns, easier letting and greater security.

CAC wished to reflect the social and planning-use mix of the local area along Caledonian Road, with the opportunity for workshops, smaller businesses, live/work units and residential, while still retaining a few more sympathetically-integrated larger buildings, namely offices and an hotel. CAC saw Albion Yard as the centre of this focus, and its retention, along with the Pontifex works, as non-negotiable. The completion of the Ironworks courtyard with a new sympathetic building on its southern side also grew from these early recommendations of CAC, and first saw light of day in these sketches.

Security at King's Cross was at that time a big local issue, especially with drugs and prostitution. The rejected scheme had planned a heavily-gated development, a response which would just force the problems back onto the streets, to the detriment of the buildings' occupants. CAC argued that a more permeable development, with a mix of uses bringing visitors throughout the day and evening, and encouraging them to enter and pass through the site via its many yards and passages, would create natural policing, and reduce crime. This was not at this period a generally accepted view. It was a great joy that the final designs adopted these ideas, for which local campaigners had been working tirelessly with the Metropolitan Police for a long time. Time has proved them right.

It was also CAC's view that the infill should not be modern "trophy" buildings, but should follow a much more sympathetic conservation approach, blending with, and stitching together, the archaeological heritage buildings.

The sketch proposals were prepared in November 2000, in consultation with Alec Forshsaw, at that time Islington's redoubtable Conservation Officer. They were by necessity very vague, and by no means perfect; it had not been possible to enter many of the buildings to assess their merits, nor did time or resources allow a detailed approach, but they formed a benchmark by which subsequent planning applications could be assessed.

They showed it could be done. Commercial expertise on CAC was also able to demonstrate that the buildings in such a development could be viable and profitable. Indeed it was argued that they would be more so than P&O's rejected scheme.

Much to everyone's surprise, a bruised P&O received these sketch proposals very positively and sympathetically, and, as we know, appointed new architects who entered enthusiastically into the conservation spirit, at a time when such an approach was still quite revolutionary for commercial development. They are truly to be commended for this, and for entering into a partnership with the community.

As the design developed P&O and their architects kept up very regular consultation with CAC, and indeed, in the closing stages before planning, on a detailed joint site visit CAC was able to suggest that the workshop behind the Jahn Building could be saved simply by turning the proposed office "atrium" through 90 degrees and using the shed for this purpose, thus saving a significant and beautiful building. It was agreed on site!

Less successful were CAC's attempts to save the interiors of the bank and other buildings along Pentonville Road, but much has been included in the design, such as the relocated Bravington's glass dome, to mitigate this loss.

Many other factors came together in this project. At the time of the CAC sketches the bus gyratory still went clockwise along Caledonia Street - the inclusion of this as a pedestrian-friendly part of the design was pure wishful thinking! It was a real surprise that the mindset at London Regional Transport and the Highways Agency should have been changing sufficiently fast at this time for P&O and their architects, supported by local lobbying, to argue this case successfully. Again, this was revolutionary, one of the first one-way systems to be reversed.

At many levels this scheme is a tribute to the open-mindedness of a commercial land developer, and to the hard work of a committed local community. It was also, we believe, a blue-print for successful collaborative urban-renewal developments in historic settings everywhere, to the benefit of everyone.

The happy results may be proved by a walk through the Regent Quarter.

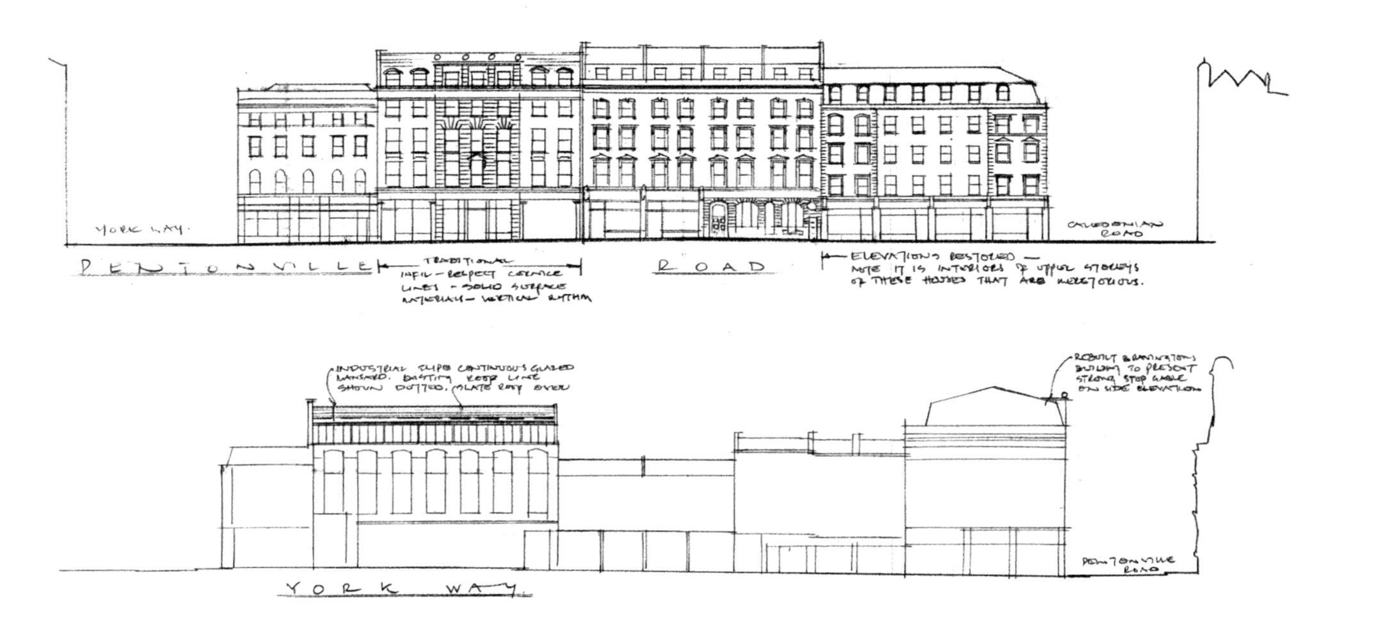

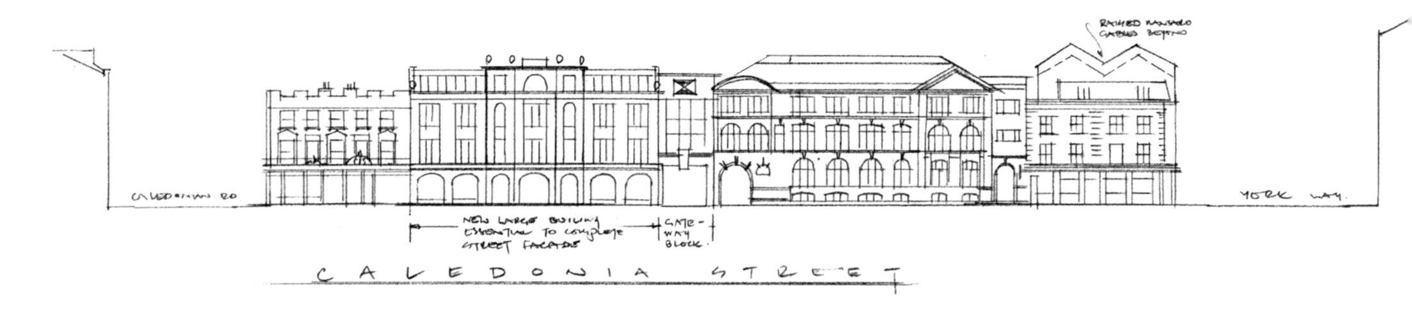

Architect's drawings of King's Cross for Islington CAC, November 2000.

Above: Block B sketch elevations.

Right: Block B plan sketch proposal.

Drawings: Anthony Delarue Associates

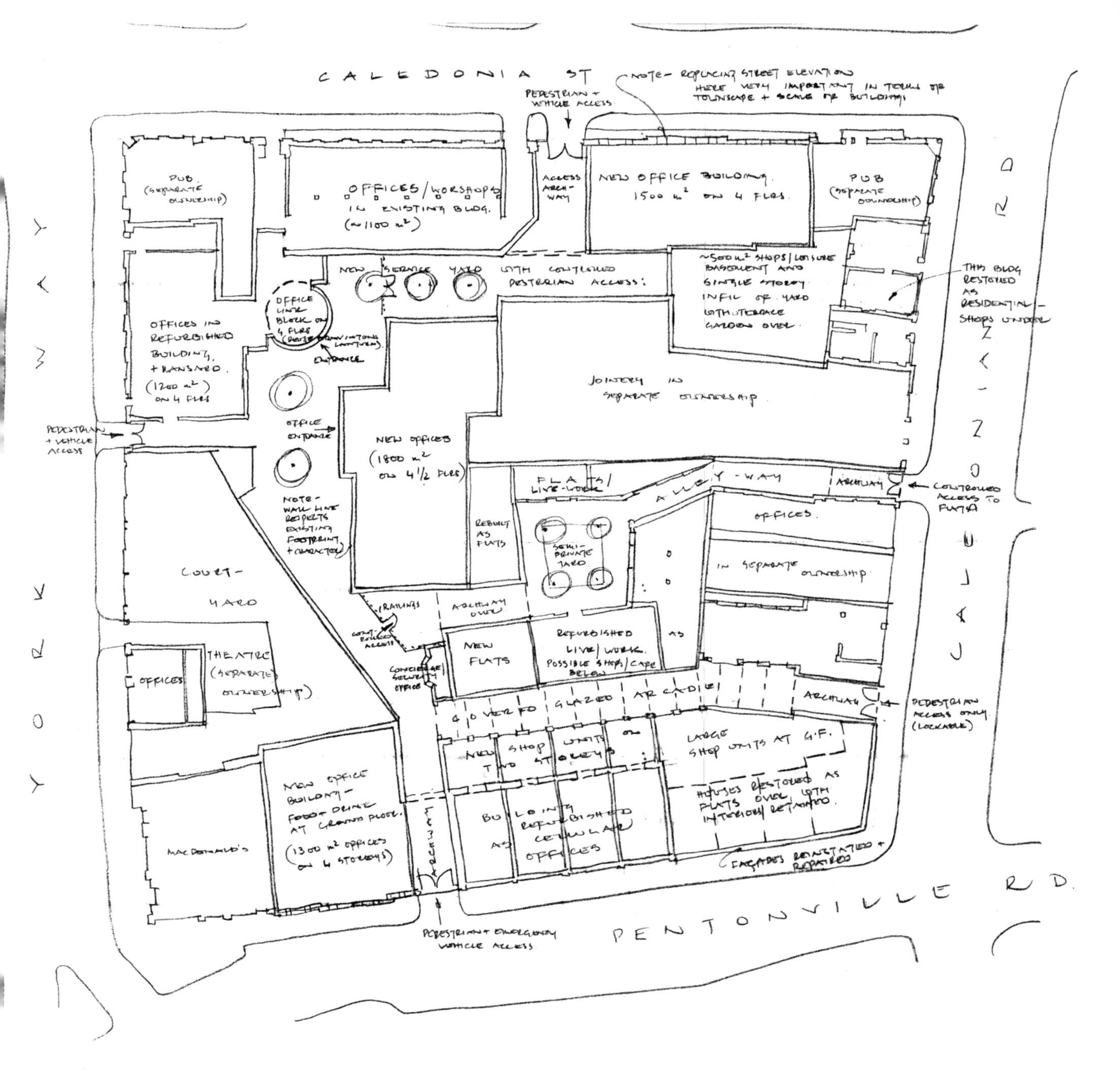
CALEDONIA ST
PEDESTRIAN + VEHICLE ACCESS
NOTE – REPLACING STREET ELEVATION HERE VERY IMPORTANT IN TERMS OF TOWNSCAPE + SCALE OF BUILDINGS
PUB (SEPARATE OWNERSHIP)
OFFICES/WORKSHOPS IN EXISTING BLDG. (~1100 m²)
ACCESS ARCH-WAY
NEW OFFICE BUILDING 1500 m² ON 4 FLRS.
PUB (SEPARATE OWNERSHIP)
NEW SERVICE YARD WITH CONTROLLED PEDESTRIAN ACCESS.
~500 m² SHOPS/LEISURE BASEMENT AND SINGLE STOREY INFIL OF YARD WITH TERRACE GARDEN OVER
THIS BLDG RESTORED AS RESIDENTIAL – SHOPS UNDER
OFFICES IN REFURBISHED BUILDING, + MANSARD. (1200 m²) ON 4 FLRS
ENTRANCE
JOINERY IN SEPARATE OWNERSHIP
PEDESTRIAN + VEHICLE ACCESS
OFFICE ENTRANCE
NEW OFFICES (1800 m² ON 4½ FLRS)
FLATS/LIVE-WORK
ALLEY-WAY
ARCHWAY
CONTROLLED ACCESS TO FLATS
NOTE – WALL LINE RESPECTS EXISTING FOOTPRINT + CHARACTER
REBUILT AS FLATS
SEMI-PRIVATE YARD
OFFICES IN SEPARATE OWNERSHIP
COURT-YARD
RAILINGS
ARCHWAY OVER
NEW FLATS
REFURBISHED AS LIVE/WORK. POSSIBLE SHOPS/CAFE BELOW
THEATRE (SEPARATE OWNERSHIP)
OFFICES
CONCIERGE/SECURITY OFFICE
COVERED GLAZED ARCADE
ARCHWAY
PEDESTRIAN ACCESS ONLY (LOCKABLE)
NEW SHOP UNITS ON TWO STOREYS
LARGE SHOP UNITS AT G.F.
NEW OFFICE BUILDING – FOOD + DRINK AT GROUND FLOOR. (1300 m² OFFICES ON 4 STOREYS)
HOUSES RESTORED AS FLATS OVER WITH INTERIORS RETAINED.
MACDONALD'S
ARCHWAY
BUILDINGS REFURBISHED AS CELLULAR OFFICES
FACADES REINSTATED + REPAIRED
PEDESTRIAN + EMERGENCY VEHICLE ACCESS.
PENTONVILLE RD.
YORK WAY
CALEDONIAN RD

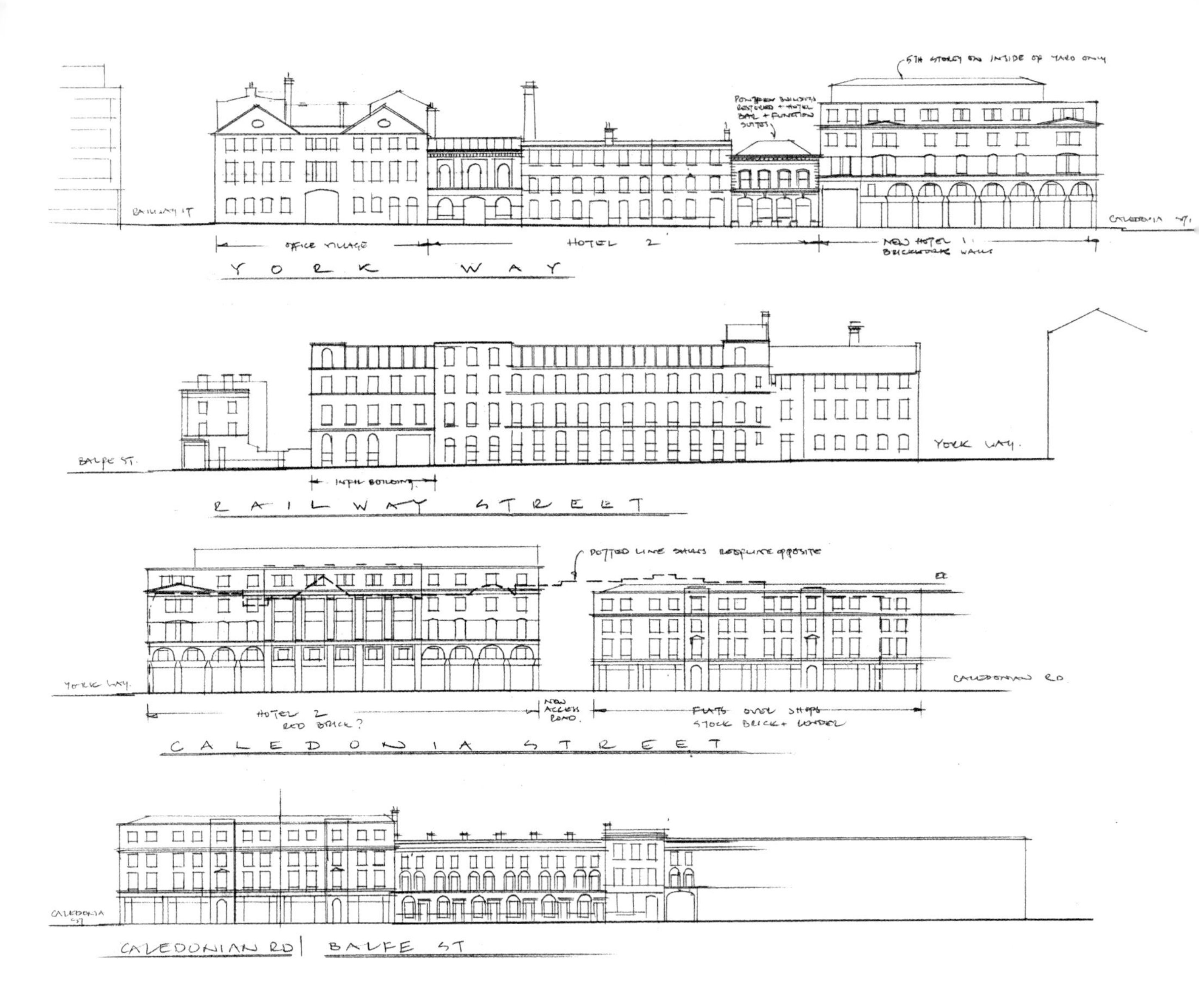

Architect's drawings of King's Cross for Islington CAC, November 2000.

Above: Block C sketch elevations.

Right: Block C plan sketch proposal.

Drawings: Anthony Delarue Associates

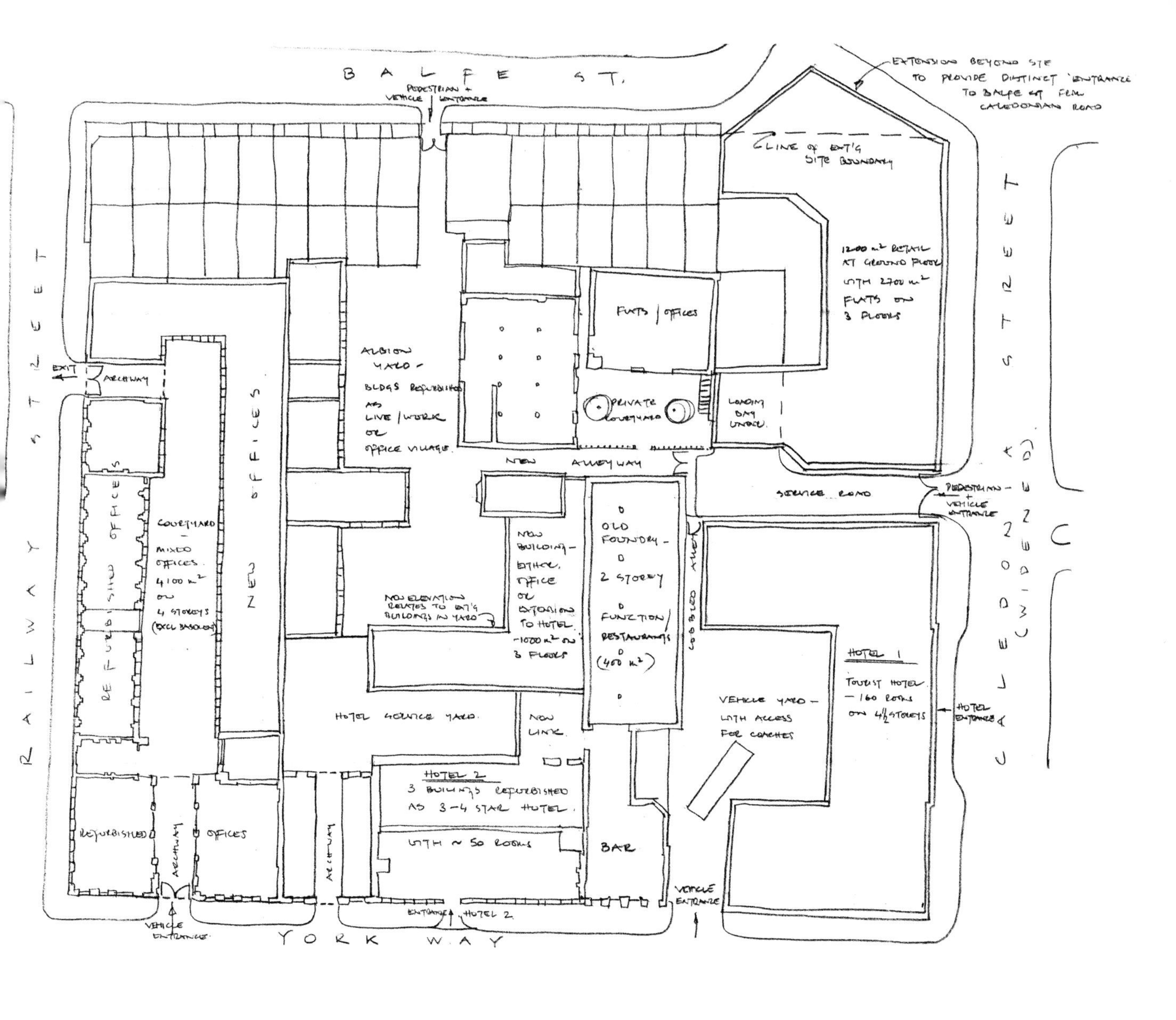
BALFE ST.
PEDESTRIAN + VEHICLE ENTRANCE
EXTENSION BEYOND SITE TO PROVIDE DISTINCT 'ENTRANCE' TO BALFE ST FROM CALEDONIAN ROAD
LINE OF EXT'G SITE BOUNDARY
1200 m² RETAIL AT GROUND FLOOR WITH 2700 m² FLATS ON 3 FLOORS
FLATS / OFFICES
ALBION YARD - BLDGS REFURBISHED AS LIVE / WORK OR OFFICE VILLAGE
PRIVATE COURTYARD
LOADING BAY UNDER
NEW ALLEY WAY
SERVICE ROAD
PEDESTRIAN + VEHICLE ENTRANCE
EXIT
ARCHWAY
NEW OFFICES
COURTYARD - MIXED OFFICES 4100 m² ON 4 STOREYS (EXCL BASEMENT)
REFURBISHED OFFICES
NEW ELEVATION RELATES TO EXT'G BUILDINGS IN YARD
NEW BUILDING - EITHER OFFICE OR EXTENSION TO HOTEL - 1000 m² ON 3 FLOORS
OLD FOUNDRY - 2 STOREY FUNCTION / RESTAURANTS (400 m²)
COBBLED ALLEY
HOTEL 1
TOURIST HOTEL - 160 ROOMS ON 4½ STOREYS
HOTEL ENTRANCE
VEHICLE YARD - WITH ACCESS FOR COACHES
HOTEL SERVICE YARD
NEW LINK
HOTEL 2
3 BUILDINGS REFURBISHED AS 3-4 STAR HOTEL
WITH ~ 50 ROOMS
BAR
REFURBISHED
ARCHWAY
OFFICES
ARCHWAY
VEHICLE ENTRANCE
ENTRANCE HOTEL 2
VEHICLE ENTRANCE
YORK WAY
RAILWAY STREET
TREST
CALEDONIAN ROAD

Maiden Lane

Artist: E. H. Dixon 1835 watercolour.
View northwards from the canal.
Painting: Courtesy Islington Local History Centre

Part Two:

The industrial legacy of Battle Bridge

Battlebridge Basin

Kings Place

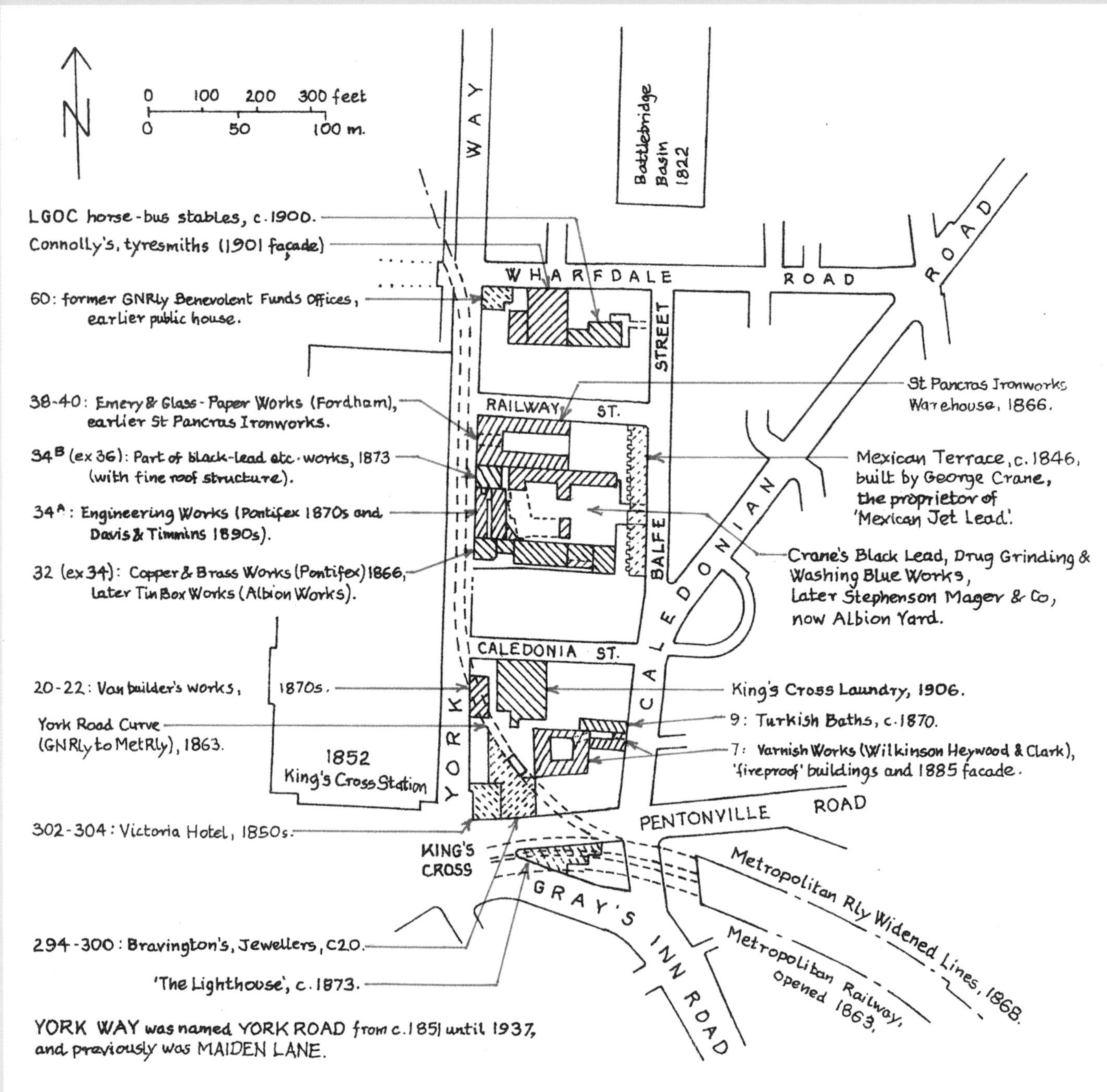

The P&O Blocks: former commercial premises in 1990

Chapter 4

The industrial legacy of Battle Bridge

Regent Quarter's earlier history

with narration and photographs by Malcolm Tucker

Where was Battle Bridge?

Battle Bridge was a hamlet next to where the road from Gray's Inn to St Pancras and Kentish Town crossed the River Fleet. In the middle ages it was Bradford Bridge, and there is no foundation for the story that it marked where the rebellious Queen Boudicca was defeated in battle by the Romans.[1] The River Fleet was covered over here around 1800.

Going northwards from the bridge, and forming the ancient boundary between St Pancras and Islington parishes, was an old road called Maiden Lane. The romantic-sounding name was perhaps derived from muddy or from midden – it is now York Way. From the south-east, another road (now King's Cross Road) came up the Fleet valley from the City and where this passed east-west through Battle Bridge the New Road from Paddington to the Angel was also squeezed through, under an Act of 1756 which created London's first by-pass road.[2] The Islington portion of the New Road was renamed Pentonville Road in 1857. The name King's Cross was invented in 1830 for the point where these several routes meet, to promote the neighbourhood to its south.[3] A monument to the late King George IV was then erected at the centre of the cross roads, but it was short-lived.[4]

A further road, from Battle Bridge to Holloway, was built as a toll road under an Act of 1826, meeting the New Road 100 yards or so east of Maiden Lane. It was called at first the Chalk Road and then the Caledonian Road.

Map: Malcolm T. Tucker

To its east, Pentonville was already built up with houses, but in the area of this study, westward from Caledonian Road, such development was very slow until the 1840s, perhaps because of the unsavoury reputation of the Fleet valley.[5]

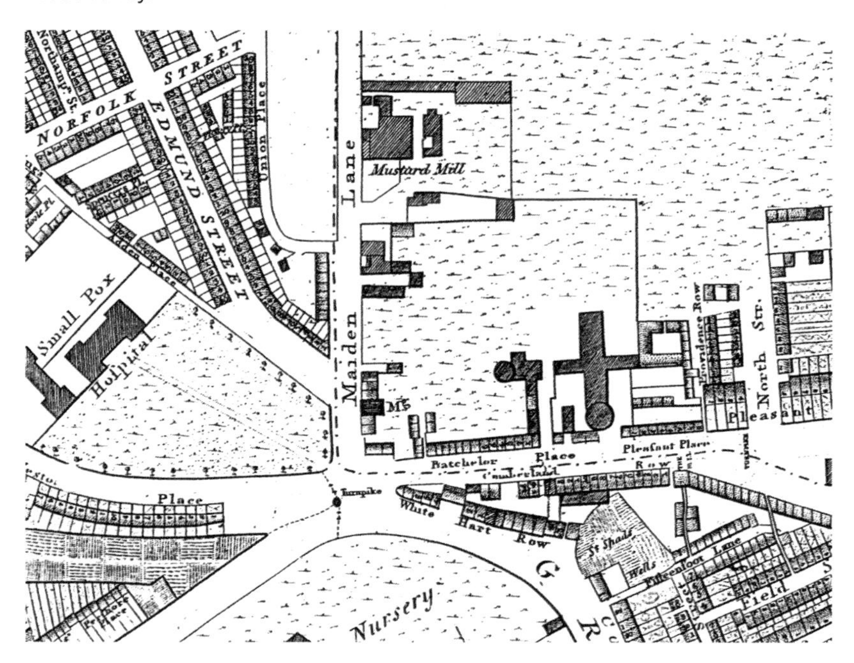

1819 edition of Harwood's map showing the mustard mill on Maiden Lane

In this Islington portion of Battle Bridge, east of Maiden Lane, buildings had started to appear on the map by 1800, including a terrace of houses on the New Road of which some still remain and a cluster of buildings about 180 yards up Maiden Lane that by 1819 was labelled as Mustard Mill.[6] Other trades established here at that period included bone merchants, slaughterers, a soap boiler, a pottery, manufacturers of coach grease, chemicals, varnish and paints and a firm dressing feathers for bedding.[7] Some of these relatively 'noisome' industries were to characterise this area, and the satellite industrial colony that developed further north at Belle Isle, until the 20th century.

About the layout of this chapter

The following pages will describe the industrial and commercial historic buildings in the area now partly rebuilt and partly refurbished as the 'Regent Quarter', which is bounded by Caledonian Road, Pentonville Road, York Way, Wharfdale Road and Balfe Street, to use their modern names, plus the block on the south side of Pentonville Road nicknamed the 'Lighthouse Block'. The latter was owned in the 1990s by the same company as developed the Regent Quarter, P&O Properties, and their labelling of the blocks from south to north is useful for present purposes, viz. Block 'A' the Lighthouse Block, Block 'B' from Pentonville Road to Caledonia Street, Block 'C' from Caledonia Street to Railway Street and Block 'D' from Railway Street to Wharfdale Road. However, the account will commence with the oldest surviving site, now known as Albion Yard within Block 'C'. From the premises around Albion Yard it will work northwards through Block 'D' and southwards again through Block 'B' to Block 'A'. The chapter will conclude with some comments on how the recent developments have come about, as described and illustrated in more detail in the preceding chapter.

The Black Lead, Washing Blue and Drug Grinding Mills – present Albion Yard

The mill already mentioned that ground mustard and also 'stone' blue was acquired around 1831 by George Crane, a blue maker and drug grinder previously in St Luke's and the City.[8] By 1839 he had passed on the business to Stephenson, Mager and Co., who later described themselves as 'importers of black lead & sole proprietors of George Crane's celebrated Mexican jet lead, blue mfrs, drug and spice grinders etc.'[9]. In this instance the black lead (i.e. graphite) was probably obtained in a rock-like form, so it was crushed and ground under the heavy edge-runner stones that characterised these mills and then sold as a powder or reconstituted into blocks for polishing grates and stoves. Stone blue was the term for the vegetable dye indigo, imported in lumps and needing to be ground before mixing with starch for sale as a laundry whitener.

The mills were centred in a large rectangular plot on the east side of Maiden Lane (numbered 10 Maiden Lane in 1832), but a railway survey of 1846 showed this in a state of change.[10] Along the eastern boundary, an as yet unoccupied terrace of houses had been built by George Crane

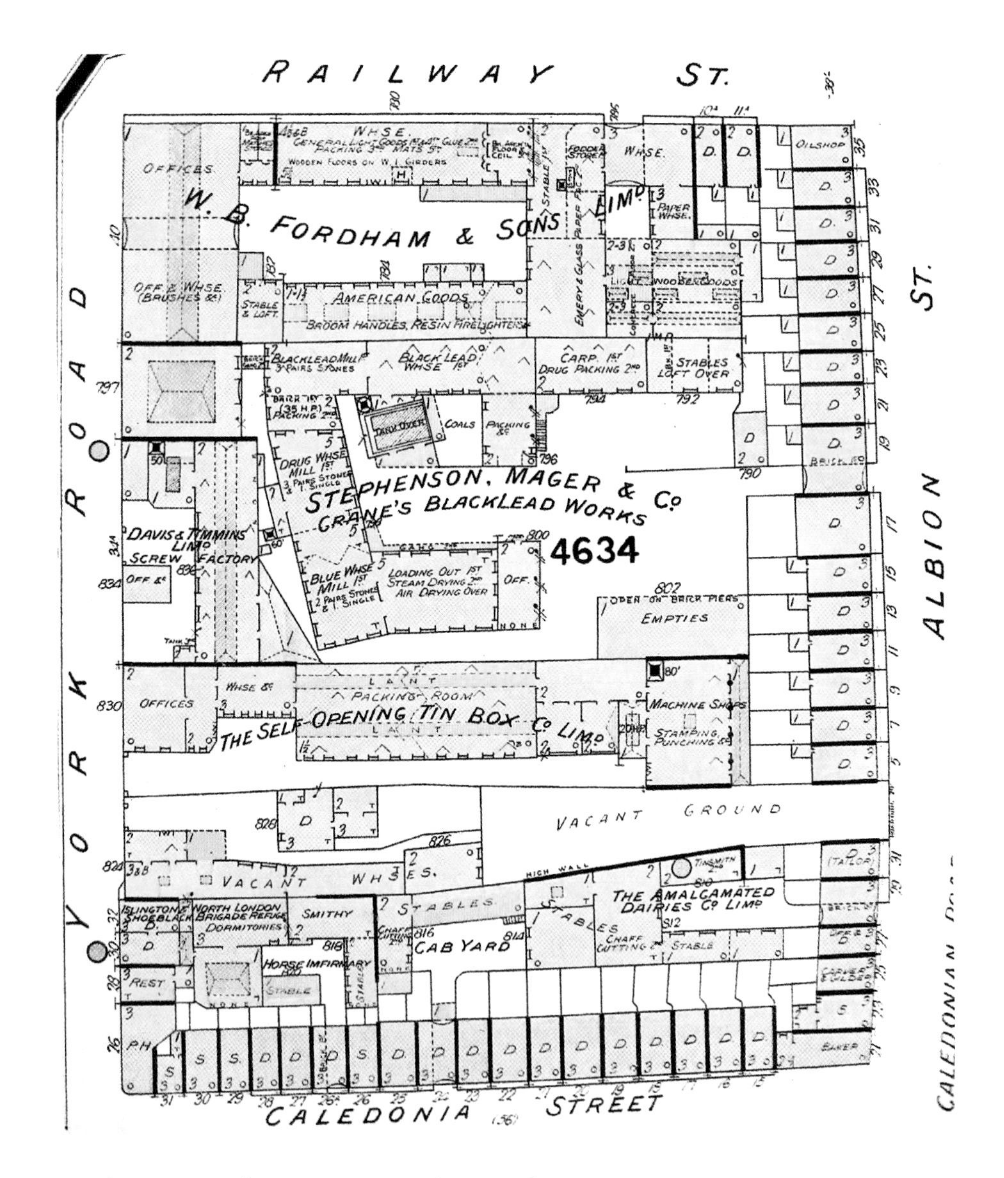

Goad Insurance Plan XII-393, March 1891, showing the buildings then standing in what became Block 'C'.

facing the new Albion Street. These appeared in the rate books from 1847 as Mexican Terrace, presumably commemorating Crane's successful 'jet lead' product – they are now Nos. 5-35 Balfe Street. The archway through still carries the inscriptions "WORKS & MILLS" and "1846", although it was at first obstructed by an older building behind. The substantial house next to it (now No. 17) was presumably for the works manager. On the opposite boundary the works still fronted Maiden Lane, and it was not until the late 1850s that the office address was moved to Albion Street. Maiden Lane was renamed York Road soon after 1850, when the Great Northern Railway's goods station and temporary passenger station were opened just north of the canal. In 1852 the passenger station was opened on its present site. These events gave a strong boost to the area's commercial prospects. York Road was renamed York Way in 1937, while Albion Street became Balfe Street in 1938.[11]

Over the next few years, the "Black Lead Works" was shrunk to a more compact, inner-block arrangement, allowing some peripheral land to be redeveloped.[12] The new layout with 2-storey buildings around a yard remained relatively unaltered, except for some demolitions, until its recent reconfiguration as part of the 'Regent Quarter'. Details are shown on the Insurance Plan of 1891 (see Figure).[13] In the northern range, built circa 1850, the Black Lead Mill and Warehouse were located towards the western end, now gone, while the still surviving eastern part and the central, southward-projecting wing (with the broad arched doorway and wall crane) housed packing operations and stables for delivery horses. Opposite was the Office, which can still be recognised from the oriel window that allowed surveillance. At the west end of the yard was a range set obliquely to the other buildings, which had existed in 1846 and was demolished in the mid-20th century. This housed the Drug Mill, the Blue Mill and a 35 horsepower steam engine, with warehousing on the upper floor. There was also a steam drying room. The mills contained ten sets of stones, mostly in pairs and some singly, presumably all of the edge-runner type with heavy vertical stones trundling around in a tight circle upon a bed stone. They would crush relatively soft materials and, if the runner stones were made broad relative to the diameter of the bed stone, the skidding action at the edges would also grind the product by shearing, particularly useful with the fibrous vegetable ingredients of traditional drugs.

Entrance to Albion Yard from Balfe St, formerly Mexican Terrace, Albion Street, 5 March 1977.

Albion Yard, rear of image on left, 5 March 1977.

Top right: Albion Yard from the entrance in Balfe Street, 5 March 1977.

Right: Albion Yard from SW. The facing block originally housed packing operations and stables. 5 March 1977.

Far right: Albion Yard office showing oriel window, 5 March 1977.

CHAMPION
CHAMPION

An edge runner stone formerly in Albion Yard. Stones such as these were used in grinding and crushing processes.

Shortly before 1910, Stephenson, Mager and Co. sold out to Hargreaves Brothers of Hull, another black-lead and washing-blue manufacturer, and the mills then closed. Before 1914[14] a new 3-storey building was built in the south-east corner and by 1920[15] 'Albion Works, Albion Street' was occupied by miscellaneous firms. In the later 20th century it became known as 'Albion Yard' and, after demolition of the western range, it spent its last industrial days as motor repair workshops. One or two of the grinding stones were to be seen lying around the site.

In the redevelopment, 5-storey offices occupy the western half of this site, yet are hardly visible from the streets around, while the remaining buildings are now flats. Their two storeys have been raised to three, with the loss of the eaved and slated roofs, but this has allowed a more comfortable build-up of scale to the offices. Passageways have tactfully penetrated the boundary walls to north and south, while some of the grinding stones are displayed in the high quality paving.

Henry Pontifex and Sons' Albion Works

A strip of land released along the south side of the mills was occupied from 1867 by Henry Pontifex and Sons, coppersmiths and engineers, who made equipment for breweries and similar process industries.[16] Their "Albion Works" was a west-east range of buildings, labelled "Foundry (Copper & Brass)" on the 1871 Ordnance Survey. It was numbered 34 York Road from 1881 and became a part of 32 York Way in the 20th century.[17] The part now converted to architect's offices comprised an office building of 2 storeys plus basement, smartly Italianate in the front part, a 3-storey warehouse behind that and the main workshop under heavy timber roof trusses. Three small chimneys formerly against the north wall may have served hearths for annealing copper or furnaces for melting brass, while one may observe

Pontifex's works, from a commercial directory

ESSO
WASH ENTRANCE
DERV
OIL

KINGS CROSS MOTORS
JAHN
VANGUARD

JAHN
CAR WASH 60p

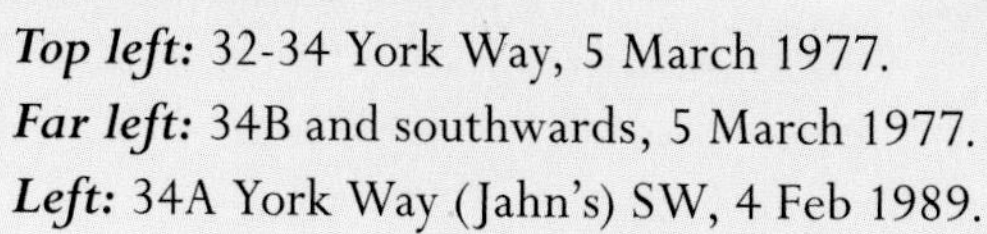

Top left: 32-34 York Way, 5 March 1977.
Far left: 34B and southwards, 5 March 1977.
Left: 34A York Way (Jahn's) SW, 4 Feb 1989.

Top: Albion Works 32 (ex-34) York Way from SE, 1 Aug 1996.
Top right: Albion Works 32 (ex-34) York Way from ESE, 30 Oct 2002.
Right: Hand winch for crane, rear warehouse of Albion Works, top floor from SE, 1 Aug 1996.

high-level windows for ventilation in the south wall, a round ventilation opening in the west gable and a tall opening below that for sending out the huge vessels formed from copper sheet that would have been made here. Casting brass fittings was only an incidental part of the firm's activities, so the modern name "The Brassworks" would seem to be erroneous. Eastwards were some less substantial workshops, now replaced by an attractive courtyard, and a 3-storey building with industrial chimney and wall crane at the east end of the site, converted into flats. The hand-operated winch for the crane is now displayed at ground level.

Pontifex seem to have left York Road around 1883 and for 25 years from 1886 the Albion Works was occupied by the Self Opening Tin Box Company (their patent being for the kind of lid one finds on paint cans).[18] They inserted an upper floor in the workshop. From the 1920s to the 1990s this site was mostly occupied by taxi-cab repairers, with various uses in the rear part, but the buildings remained little altered. The office/studio conversion of the P&O scheme has respected this integrity, and the inserted floor has largely been removed to reveal the roof structure.

Hipped roof structure at 34B York Way (see photo, page 113)

Northwards up York Way: the north-west part of 'Block C'

The plot alongside York Road immediately to the north of Albion Works lay vacant for some years from the 1850s. An extension of the Pontifex copper works was erected here at some time after 1871, with a tall two-storey building set slightly back from the road and ranged north-south. Its heavy timber roof has been incorporated into the new office block that now backs onto Albion Yard, with the lower floors removed to create an atrium. Some panels of a sectional cast-iron water tank bearing the name HENRY PONTIFEX & SONS are displayed there. In a yard alongside the street there was originally a boiler house, of which the chimney has been preserved as a feature in the office forecourt.[19] Around 1893-4, during the occupation of Davis and Timmins Ltd, screw manufacturers, a 3-storey office building was built to fill the yard.[20] It is remembered by the name of the Swedish machinery importers who succeeded them in the 1940s, Jahn, which was formerly emblazoned across the facade. The site was then known as 34A York Way. The southern half of this building has been retained and adapted as part of the new office block.[21]

Next again northwards up York Road, a small plot remained unoccupied until 1873, when Stephenson and Mager built a 2-storey warehouse for their black lead mills,[22] later numbered 34B. Behind its heavily modelled street façade, this has a remarkable hipped roof structure, of timber rafters trussed three-dimensionally with iron in such a way that half the weight of the roof is conveyed to the four corners of the building. It was spot-listed in 2001, which was one of the factors contributing to the rethinking of proposals for the redevelopment of this block, and it has been successfully converted to a business meetings centre.

Forming the northern side of this street block, where the 1846 survey showed vacant building ground, the St Pancras Ironwork Company built a corrugated ironworks and a foundry in the mid 1850s.[23] Cast-iron beams in the former loading bay of the 4-storey warehouse remaining here carry their name, with the date "ERECTED A.D. 1866". The red-striped brickwork on the ground floor of this building along Edward (now Railway) Street continues round the corner of York Way in the offices, originally of a single storey, with an arched entrance to the works.[24] The ironworks company left this site around 1875, to be succeeded by WB Fordham & Son, emery and glass-paper manufacturers and general hardware dealers.[25] Fordham's added two more storeys to the ironworks offices around 1900 and remained there until the 1930s, when Meakers the men's outfitters took over much of the premises.[26] Such other buildings as survived bomb damage here were of little note. The street-side buildings have been retained as offices and flats, flanking the original courtyard.

'Block D'

We next consider the block northwards to Wharfdale Road. The road on its south side was shown laid out but unnamed on the 1846 railway survey, but soon it became Edward Street and then, in the 1880s, it was renamed Railway Street to distinguish it from the many other Edward Streets in London.[27] Its north and east sides originated in the 1820s as tracks giving access to Mr Horsfall's canal basin (see Chapter 5), then becoming Wharf Road on the north (renamed Wharfdale Road in 1868) and Albion Street on the east (renamed Balfe Street in 1938).[28] Probably after the extraction of clay for brick making, which lowered the ground levels, the previously agricultural land was built up around 1850 with terraces of houses and mews yards behind them. To confuse matters, one of these was named Albion Yard (unrelated to the black lead and washing blue site). Along York Road there were small shops and tradesmen, with a few buildings already shown on an 1844 railway survey. A neat corner pub at No. 60, The Ambassador, was taken over in the early 20th century by the Great Northern Railway for their staff benevolent funds office. Recently it has been altered as a sandwich bar and P&O have added a mansard roof for increased residential accommodation above.

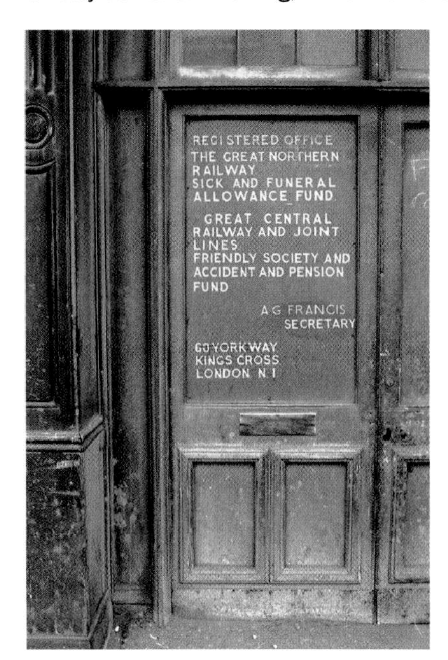

Former railway benevolent funds office in 1977

Stall partitions in the horse-bus stables, 55 Balfe Street, 2001

Industry made its appearance first in the yards behind Wharfdale Road, including a tyresmith's and a wheelwright's, and invaded the remaining yards during the 20th century.[29] A remarkable survivor behind 55 Balfe Street is the two-storeyed stables for the London General Omnibus Company, built around the year 1900 when motor buses were hardly in sight. As was usual at the time, a ramp gave access to the upper level to save on land. Some stall partitions remain where they guard a subsidiary ramp, their end posts bearing a lion's head and the initials LGOCo. Redevelopment for flats is in progress at the time of writing on the redundant sites within this block, but retaining the industrial façade at 57-63 Wharfdale Road (built for the tyresmiths, JW&T Connolly) and the facade of the c.1850 terrace at 39-51. The stables, listed Grade 2 since 2001, are being adapted as studio offices.

Southwards, into 'Block B'

Before the redevelopment, the south edge of Block 'C' where the hotel now stands was very run-down. 32 York Way was an ugly taxi repair garage from c.1920, yet that site, at one time 9 Maiden Lane, had previously been occupied by one of the oldest businesses in the area, the feather bed manufacturers and feather dressers JY Rood and Co. They were there in 1811 and still there 100 years later.[30] No 30 next-door was another large motor garage, on the site of the dormitories of the Islington and North London Shoe Black Brigade and Refuge of 1868. No.28 retained an early-nineteenth-century Georgian facade, very grimy. Around the corner in Caledonia Street, behind a terrace of houses that was demolished in the 1950s, had been yards full of jobmaster's stables, with a smithy and a horse infirmary.[31] The glazed roof over a new passage behind Tesco's store has been relocated from the former Bravington's premises at 296-298 Pentonville Road.

Caledonia Street with its houses was drawn and named on the railway survey of 1846 but not on a survey of two years previously.[32] To its south, Block 'B' had a denser and more irregular grain of buildings, having started its development earlier and with more occasions for piecemeal rebuilding. For instance the now disused York Road railway curve, connecting the Great Northern Railway to the Metropolitan Railway, was driven through its south-western part in 1862, partly in retained cutting and partly in cut-and-cover tunnel. So, whereas the east part of the Pentonville Road frontage of the block may have been late 18th-century, the grander part next to it at Nos. 286-292, which included the National Bank, was a post-railway rebuilding of c.1870. This part of the site was considerably re-formed behind the retained facades in the recent development. Westward again was the well-known jeweller's shop, Bravington's, with a facade rebuilt in the mid-C20 and extensive showrooms from the early 20th century at the back.[33] This has been totally rebuilt, but a domed lantern has been saved and re-erected on a new building further to the east and another glazed roof is now in Block C as already noted. On the corner facing King's Cross, the building with a handsome cornice was built in the early 1850s as the Victoria Hotel, in response to the main-line railway's arrival, while the more eclectically 'Victorian' row of shops to its north replaced some of the earliest developed plots along Maiden Lane.

The smart 'warehouse' now refurbished as offices at 20-22 York Way was still a cleared site over the railway curve in 1871 – later a van-builder and wheelwright's workshops occupied the ground floor and a rear yard, with dressmakers' workshops over.[34]

Boiler chimney of King's Cross Laundry in 2001

On the corner of Caledonia Street is a 1920s-rebuilt old pub, followed by the red-brick, mildly Baroque facade of the King's Cross Laundry, dated 1906, which adds further to the local mix of styles. This had rambling, top-lit laundry rooms to its rear before the redevelopment. On the Caledonian Road frontage of the block, the 4-storey Georgian-style terrace of shops started construction in the 1830s, but some of the facades are modern pastiche. At No. 9, a Turkish bath suite was built circa 1870 and closed in 1921 and there are remains of the bath boarded over.[35] The most interesting site in this block is No. 7 Caledonian Road, the former premises of Wilkinson, Heywood and Clark, colour and varnish manufacturers. It has a tile-hung, Arts-and-Crafts-style façade of 1885 by architects Romaine-Walker and Tanner,[36] listed Grade 2 in 1981, while the works was in the yard behind and protected by the same listing under curtilage rules. The works was already there in 1871 but it was evidently re-planned and largely rebuilt before 1894, using fireproof brick jack arches upon wrought-iron beams.[37] This construction was occasioned by the highly flammable product, and the proprietors apprehensively refused admission to the surveyor making the fire insurance plan for this block in 1892.[38] These attractively irregular buildings have been retained and refurbished as "Varnisher's Yard".

Varnish works entrance from Caledonian Road, 4 May 1985.

Varnish works passageway from Caledonian Road, 4 May 1985.

Varnish works, SE corner of yard, 10 Feb 1996.

The 'Lighthouse' Block

Islington parish extended locally south to Gray's Inn Road until the mid nineteenth century, when the boundary with St Pancras parish was rationalised to the centreline of Pentonville Road.[39] So the 'Lighthouse' Block is now in the London Borough of Camden.

Gray's Inn Road and Pentonville Road converge at an very acute angle, creating a site of classic 'flat-iron' shape. Already by 1814 the 'White Hart' public house had adopted a semi-circular plan to exploit the apex of the site and subsequent buildings perpetuated the idea, culminating in the present building of the early 1870s that has earned the modern 'Lighthouse' nickname.[40] This block has the further distinction of being almost entirely underlain by railway lines, namely the original two tracks of

View of the 'Lighthouse' in 1985

the Metropolitan underground line opened in 1863 and their duplication on the north side by the 'City Widened Lines', completed in 1868 and now a part of the 'Thameslink' route. The site had therefore to be entirely cleared for the construction of two brick-barrelled tunnels by the 'cut and cover' method and then redeveloped. The buildings that were erected have wrought-iron plate girders below basement level to spread their weight evenly across the tunnels and the surrounding ground.[41]

The main building was a commercial development of individual shops with general accommodation over, completed circa 1873.[42] It rises at the narrow western end to four storeys, not counting the non-functional 'lighthouse' tower of zinc-clad timber that rises a further two storeys as an eye-catcher at the apex of the block. The Italian Renaissance architecture, although routine in style, was quite daintily arranged to make the 'lighthouse' the climax of the block, with the walls diminishing eastwards to three storeys below dormer windows and tall chimneys. These enlivened the streetscape, until the commencement in 2011 of major reconstruction works as noted below. Along Gray's Inn Road, the façade was cut short by the hall of the former London Cabmen's Mission, erected at the same time.[43] A Metropolitan Railway station entrance building stood to the east but made way for a new road (King's Cross Bridge) that was cut through in 1910 for the benefit of the tramways, leaving a ragged termination of the block at that end. The one-time King's Cross Cinema, completed in 1914, dominates the opposite side above the busy traffic.

The 'Lighthouse' has attracted considerable attention and in 1997 it was listed at Grade 2 as an important local landmark, the designation being confined to the short 4-storey portion rather than the whole range of the building.

As 'Block A', this site was one of the properties that P&O Properties acquired from Stock Conversion and in 2002 they submitted a scheme for replacing the building's congested interior, of brick cross walls, timber floors and numerous staircases, by open-planned office floors within the retained facades.[44] Although Camden Council were minded to approve, subject to monetary contributions for social purposes under a 'Section 106' agreement, P&O decided it was commercially unviable – there was relatively little floor area relative to the expense of reconstruction – and they sold it on to another company. Emptied of its tenants and with zero maintenance, the building was rapidly becoming an eyesore. In 2008, UK Real Estate Ltd obtained consent for a less sensitive scheme, with extra floors and plant rooms within a bulbous rooftop extension, which is now proceeding.[45]

The Regent Quarter project

The King's Cross area suffered relative decline through the 20th century, as industries moved away and the building stock grew older and more grimy. This was perhaps exacerbated in later years by the fashion for comprehensive redevelopment. The property company Stock Conversion & Investment Trust assembled extensive holdings of land here, but never complete blocks, before they sold them on to P&O Properties Ltd in the mid 1980s.[46] Stock Conversion had already obtained some long lasting consents in 1983, particularly for redevelopment on either side of Caledonia Street, but they wer never implemented. A temporary postponement of development aspirations arose because of British Rail's promotion in 1989 of a high-speed railway link from the Channel Tunnel, which would pass under central London in a tunnel and terminate, for the moment, in an interchange station excavated on the diagonal beneath the existing King's Cross Station. (See Chapter 2). The project would require surface sites to provide the contractors' accommodation and access to the tunnelling works. A large area of land considered to be in marginal uses was designated for that and conditional demolition consents were obtained, imposing a blight on the area. Although this was overtaken by the alternative scheme to route the line via Stratford into St Pancras Station, it was not until that was confirmed in the Channel Tunnel Rail Link Act of 1996 that developers were again free to move forward with proposals. They were then still recovering from the recession of 1991.

Islington Planning Department had kept a keen interest in the borough's historic building stock, undertaking a local listing survey in 1978. In 1986, the Greater London Council, as the authority then responsible, designated Islington's King's Cross Conservation Area, taking in all the industrial areas covered by this chapter. (They had previously designated the Keystone

Crescent Conservation Area for the residential terraces further east). In 1989, Islington drew up a planning brief for the three street blocks, calling for the retention of buildings of interest. In 2000, P&O put in planning applications through their subsidiary Charlwood Alliance Holdings Ltd for the mixed rebuilding and adaptation of their properties in Blocks 'B' , 'C' and 'D', for residential, retail and office accommodation.[47]

The architects and planners for this were Rolfe Judd. Their proposals for Block 'B' were mostly as has been built, but considerable opposition was aroused over Block 'C', not least to the proposed demolition of several key locally listed industrial buildings including the Pontifex works. As a result, RHWL Architects were appointed to make new proposals there (with Derek Lovejoy Partnership as landscape consultants). The revised scheme was approved in 2002 and work in Blocks 'B' and 'C' and a small part of Block 'D' was mostly completed in 2006. There has been acclaim all round for the way in which new buildings have been discreetly introduced in both blocks while retaining much old fabric, with pedestrian alleys and spaces wending through. RHWL are also the architects for the Block 'D' scheme as amended in 2008, which started on site in 2011.[48]

---

[1] Victoria County History, *Middlesex*, Volume 8, Islington.

[2] 29GeoII, c.88.

[3] Robert Leon, 'The Man who made King's Cross', *Camden History Review*, 17 (1992), pp.13-16.

[4] *ibid.*

[5] Land ownership may have played its part. Previously a part of Henry Penton's estate, Battle Bridge was in the freehold ownership of William Horsfall, who developed the canal basin immediately to the north. See Richard Dent's survey of Islington, 1805-6, Islington Local History Library. For a more general overview of the area's history, see Gavin Stamp, 'From Battle Bridge to King's Cross: Urban Fabric and Change', in M. Hunter and R. Thorne (eds), *Change at King's Cross,* London, Historical Publications, 1990, pp. 10-39

[6] Richard Horwood, *A Plan of the Cities of London and Westminster..*, 1797, and subsequent editions revised by William Faden, 1807, 1813, 1819.

[7] Richard Dent, Survey plan of Islington, 1806; John Nelson, *The History of Islington*, 1811 and 1829; Islington rate books; trades directories.

[8] Robson's, Pigot's and Kelly's directories, various years.

[9] Kelly's London Post Office Directory for 1877, Commercial section.

[10] Great Northern Railway Deviations Bill, Deposited Plan KCD No.2, Nov 1846, London Metropolitan Archives, MR/UP/330 (document 'unfit' at time of writing). The railway was seeking an alternative site for the King's Cross terminal station to avoid the cost and delay of relocating the Smallpox and Fever Hospitals.

[11] York Way to distinguish it from the York Road that ran past the then County Hall in Lambeth.

[12] Edward Stanford, Six-Inch Map of London, 1862; Ordnance Survey, 5 feet to 1 mile, London, Sheet VII-33, first edition, surveyed 1871; *ibid.*, 2nd edition, revised 1893-4.

[13] Charles E. Goad, Insurance Plan, London, Vol. XII, Sheet 398, March 1891.

[14] Ordnance Survey, 1:2500, London, sheet V.6, revised 1914.

[15] Kelly's Directories

[16] Kelly's London Post Office Directory for 1867, Commercial and Streets sections. Among Pontifex's products were machines for ice-making to Reece's successful patent of 1867, whereby compressed ammonia gas was absorbed into water followed by evaporation causing intense cooling, which eventually drove out natural ice such as was stored at Battlebridge Basin - see Chapter 5.

[17] Metropolitan Board of Works minute of 17 June 1881 and Renumbering Plan No. 2665/1, London Metropolitan Archives, AR/BA/5/186; Kelly's Directories.

[18] David Willis, *Nacanco Limited*, GLIAS Newsletter 96, Feb 1985.

[19] Insurance Plan XII-398, 1891, *op. cit.*

[20] Ordnance Survey 5 feet to 1 mile, revised 1893-4; 1:2500, revised 1914; Kelly's directories.

[21] The truncation of this building reverted to a short-lived earlier footprint, of which the end wall was revealed by the demolition.

[22] Joanna Smith, *34B York Way, N1*, unpublished report, English Heritage, 2000. The architects in 1873 were Thomas Marsh Nelson and William Harvey.

[23] Kelly's, various editions; Stanford, 1862; Ordnance Survey, 1871.

[24] Kelly's London Suburban (North) Directory for 1884, Advertisements section, p.42, 'W. B. Fordham & Sons', with illustration.

[25] Kelly's directory for 1878, Commercial section, has a fuller description.

[26] Insurance Plan XII-398, revised 1939.

[27] Great Northern Railway Deviations Bill, Deposited Plan KCD No.2, 1846, *op. cit.*; Stanford, 1862;

[28] Shown by dashed lines on C & J Greenwood's map of London, surveyed 1824-6; London County Council, *Names of Streets & Places in the Administrative County of London*, 4th edn., 1955.

[29] Charles E Goad, Insurance Plan, London, Vol. XII, Sheet 399, 1891.

[30] Nelson, *The History of Islington*, 1811, p.74; street directories through to 1910.

[31] Insurance Plan XII-398, 1891, *op. cit*.

[32] Great Northern Railway Deviations Bill, Deposited Plan KCD No.2, 1846, *op. cit*.; London & York Railway Bill, Deposited Plan, Part No.1, Map No.1, Nov 1844, London Metropolitan Archives, MR/UP/232.

[33] Anne Upson, *P&O Land Holdings, King's Cross, Standing Building Assessment, Block B*, AOC Archaeology Group, unpublished report, 2000.

[34] Ordnance Survey, surveyed 1871; Charles E Goad, Insurance Plan, London, Vol. D, Sheet 8, 1892.

[35] http://www.victorianturkishbath.org/ , accessed 19/06/2011. This was not one of P&O's properties.

[36] Bridget Cherry and Nicholas Pevsner, *London 4: North*, Penguin Books, Buildings of England series, 1998, p.697.

[37] Ordnance Survey, 1893-4 revision compared with 1871 survey.

[38] Insurance Plan D-8, 1892, *op. cit*..

[39] Islington parish map, c.1828.

[40] David Hayes, *A light at King's Cross*, Camden History Review, Vol. 23 (1999), pp.13-18.

[41] Gifford and Partners, *The Lighthouse Building at King's Cross, Cultural Heritage,* Report No. 11885/R10, for UK Real Estate, Oct 2008, in LB Camden planning application 2008/5358/P.

[42] Hayes, *op. cit*., p.17.

[43] *ibid*.

[44] LB Camden, planning applications PSX0004539, LSX0004540 and CSX0004541.

[45] LB Camden, planning applications 2008/5358/P and 2008/5366/L.

[46] Michael Edwards, 'King's Cross: renaissance for whom?', in John Punter (ed.), *Urban Design, Urban Renaissance and British Cities*, London, Routledge, 2010, p.197.

[47] LB Islington, planning application P000434 and associated applications.

[48] LB Islington, planning application P080281.

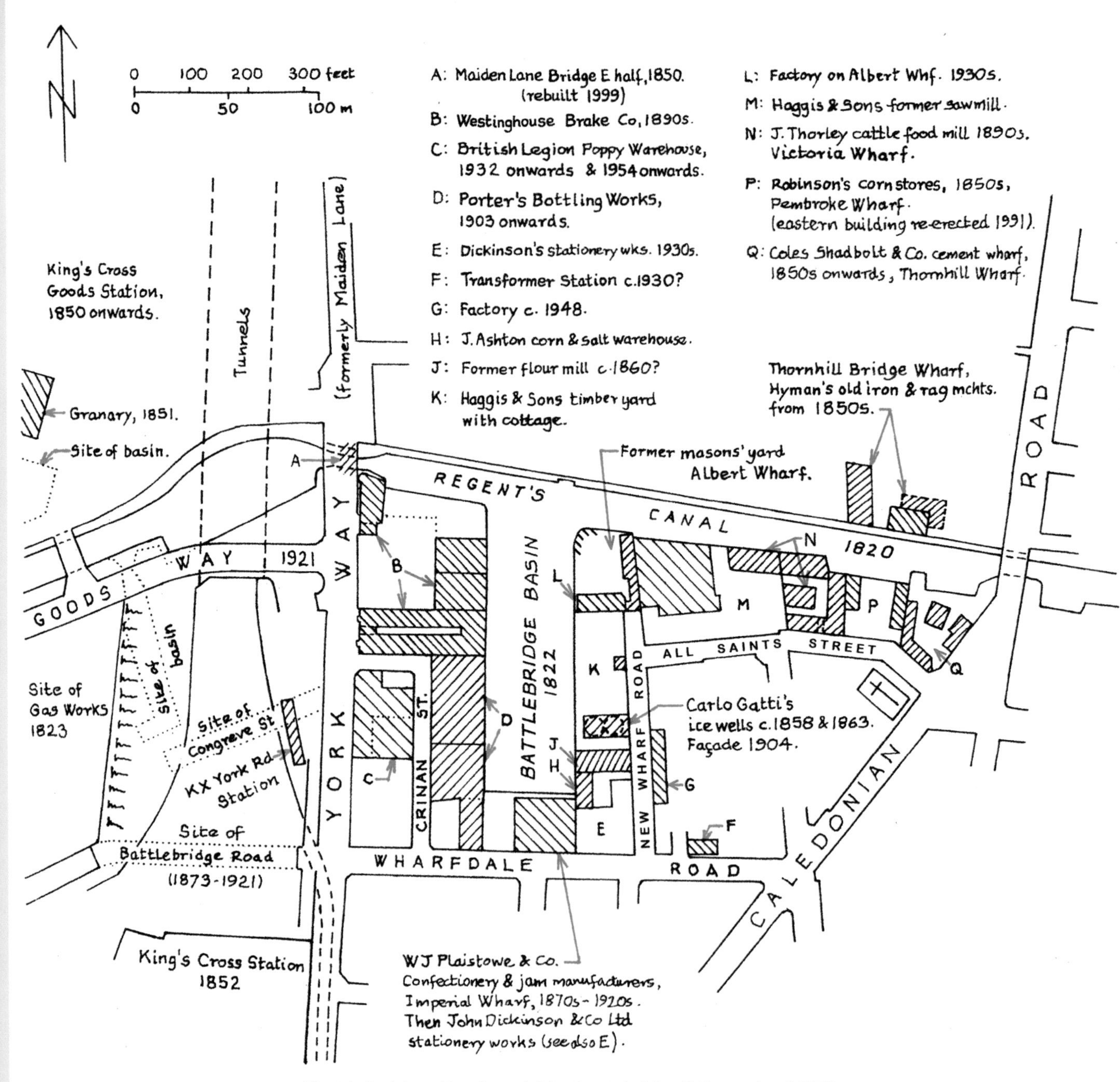

Battlebridge Basin: old industrial buildings in 1970

Chapter 5

Battlebridge Basin

Its history and development

with narration and photos by Malcolm Tucker

Introduction

Battlebridge Basin is a short, wide arm off the Regent's Canal, privately built to provide wharves where coal, building materials and other goods could be unloaded and temporarily stored, before sending on to customers by horse and cart. Constructed on the site of brickfields, it was opened in 1822. Later, warehouses and factories were built here and on the banks of the canal itself. The late twentieth century has seen these replaced by offices and housing, in new and converted buildings, with cultural attractions at the London Canal Museum and Kings Place.

The Grand Junction Canal, which connected London with the industrial Midlands, was approved by Parliament in 1793 and was fully complete in 1805.[1] Its Paddington Branch terminated at the north-western edge of London in 1801, but there had long been hopes of a canal extending from there around the northern side of the city and then down to the newly built Docks on the tidal Thames. The Regent's Canal fulfilled that dream, built by a separate company under an Act of Parliament of 1812 and completed after much financial concern and effort in 1820.[2] It carried river barges up to 14½ feet (4.4 metres) in beam as well as the Midlands narrow boats of half that width.

The canal was mostly routed through agricultural land around the fringes of town, since it was completed just before the great urban expansion of the nineteenth century. Islington village, straggling northwards, was avoided by a tunnel under the hill it stands on, dug through the London Clay that underlies most of north London and 958 yards (875 metres) long.[3]

Map: Malcolm T. Tucker

Battlebridge Basin

Building the Basin

Between Islington Tunnel and Maiden Lane (the present York Way), the Regent's Canal passed close to the land of William Horsfall.[4] The desirability of building a basin there at the company's expense was mooted in 1815, and legal provision for this basin was included in the supplementary Regent's Canal Act of 1819.[5] It was to be privately owned but subject to the requirements and regulations of the Regent's Canal Company such as safeguarding the company's water. 70 feet of land on each side of the basin (as a minimum) was to be used for wharves 'for the convenience of the public'.[6] As constructed, the basin is about 475 feet (145 metres) long and 160 feet (49 metres) wide, which allowed space for barges to turn easily and moor parallel to the sides of the basin, while the wharves extended typically 100 feet from the water's edge to the surrounding roads. The water throughout had to be at least as deep as the 5 feet (1.5 metres) depth of the main channel and, to judge from a portion that remained at 10-11 New Wharf Road until 1997, the wharf walls were originally made of timber with iron land ties.

Contructing the Islington Tunnel

The general lie of the land falls gently from north to south so that the basin, extending southwards from the canal, is constructed as an embankment and its crest is up to 7 feet (2 metres) above modern street levels. Moreover, geotechnical borehole records taken on building sites around the basin show that the present top of the London Clay is 10 to 15 feet (3 to 4.5 metres) below the modern street levels.[7] This provides evidence that the ground had been dug away to extract weathered clay suitable for making bricks and the levels were made up again. The 'made ground' with which the levels were restored is also of clay, but it contains brick fragments and layers of ash, gravel and chalk at intervals, marking temporary surfacings for the carts delivering the clay to drive over.

There was a ready source for this fill – the raw, greyish-brown clay that had been excavated from the Islington Tunnel mostly in 1814 and 1815 and had been piled in mounds near the western tunnel mouth to the embarrassment of the canal company. The slump that followed the Napoleonic War left many unemployed (and the canal company desperately short of capital), but in 1818, with the help of a government loan intended to get the economy moving again, and partly with a subsidy from the poor law trustees of St Marylebone parish, work was started to fill up Mr Horsfall's land with this clay.[8] After a few months, the experienced contractor Hugh McIntosh, who was making the western approach cutting and completing the canal westwards, was able to continue the task more effectively and complete the basin embankment.[9] There were still some unresolved matters such as access roads when the canal opened in August 1820, so it was not until April 1822 that the basin was ready for business.[10] Horsfall was evidently a hard bargainer and he seems to have got the basin built on his land and the possession of additional small land parcels free of charge.[11]

The Hinterland

The rural scene at 'Battle Bridge' at the beginning of this book, supposedly of 1812, was probably taken in the fields somewhere to the west of the later Basin. If the water in the foreground is not the River Fleet, then it is most likely in a brick pit, and piles of clay are probably seen weathering in the middle distance ready to make into bricks for the building developments which were then further to the south but marching ever northward. A few years later, that was the subject of George Cruikshank's well-known cartoon of 1829, 'London Going out of Town'.[12] This area of the Fleet valley was already the location of large dust heaps where domestic refuse was sorted and the residual ashes were reclaimed as an important ingredient of the distinctive 'London stock bricks' that characterise London's buildings.[13] The conical shapes of tile kilns were also prominent, while from 1823 the large Imperial Gas Works with its architecturally distinguished chimneys, on the south bank of the canal west of Maiden Lane, added to the smoke and other odours.[14] These are all featured, at least visually, in the Cruikshank cartoon. It is not surprising that housing development was retarded in the immediate vicinity, leaving a corridor through which the Great Northern Railway was able to penetrate in 1850, followed by the Midland Railway a little further west in 1867, so bringing more noise, soot and coal dust. Up the road at Copenhagen Fields, the City of London relocated its live cattle market in 1855, so that cattle lairs and slaughterhouses, gut scrapers and a bone mill joined Adams's tile kilns and various varnish makers at 'Belle Isle'.[15] Chapter 4 has already remarked on similar industries in Battle Bridge hamlet earlier in the century. However, the scene on page 132 of Maiden Lane just north of the canal in 1835 looks idyllic, so the deterrent effect of the smoke upon housing in Islington at that formative period was only relative, as many neat terraces still testify.

The Wharves around the Basin

The basin was often known as Horsfall's or Horsfall Basin, but also Battle Bridge Basin, while street directories and others called it King's Cross Basin in the mid 19th century. The Ordnance Survey maps, since 1874, have named it Battlebridge Basin, a continuing reminder of the district's former name (see Chapter 4). The Basin was well placed to meet the needs for coal and building materials of the populous and industrious areas to the south and subsequent developments to the north.

Early occupiers were nearly all coal merchants, some dealing also in gravel for roads, builders' lime and manure (as a return load). Two of the area's many dust contractors had wharves here.[16] A railway survey of 1844 shows open yards flanked by irregular ranges of buildings that would have provided superintendents' cottages, offices and covered storage.[17] A mid-19th-century wharf cottage remained at 16 New Wharf Road until the 1970s.

By the 1870s, there was a much greater diversity of premises around the basin – timber and masons' yards, saw mills for timber, stone and marble, an iron foundry, a grain and salt warehouse, a depot for imported ice and a 5½-storey, steam-driven flour mill.[18] The timber yards and saw mills handled some of the large amount of softwood timber that was imported from north-east Europe, particularly into the Surrey Docks. There it was transferred into lighters (dumb barges) for distribution throughout London's waterways, and this traffic lasted until the Surrey Docks closed

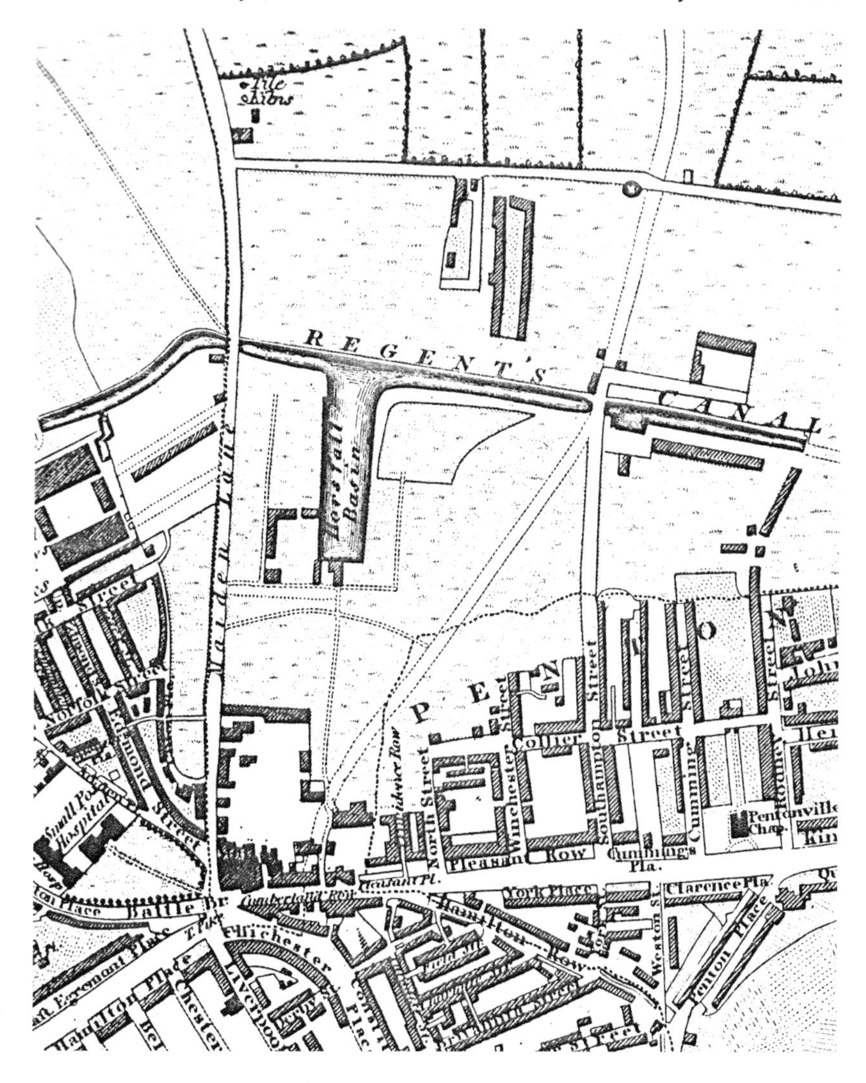

From Greenwood's map, surveyed 1824-6

Cottage of timber yard at 16 New Wharf Road, 1973

in 1970. Haggis & Sons' timber yard at 16 New Wharf Road was shown full of deals (sawn Baltic timber), stood on end 30 to 70 feet high, in 1891.[19] The flour mill at 10 New Wharf Road probably reflected the proximity of the Great Northern Railway's large Granary, erected in 1851 for corn brought to London from Eastern England and facing its own canal basin in the Goods Yard on the other side of Maiden Lane. The mill was disused by 1891, owing to major technical advances in the industry, but the building survived as a warehouse until c.1970.[20]

Carlo Gatti's ice depot, one of several such facilities in various ownership along the canal, was established on the site of a saw mill in 1857-8, at what is now 12-13 New Wharf Road (the London Canal Museum). One and then two very large ice wells were excavated into the London Clay, 34 feet in diameter and 42 feet deep (10.4m x 12.8 m). At this particular site, the ice was also stored above ground in the building over the ice wells. Blocks of ice were brought from Norway and transferred to lighters in the Regent's Canal Dock for conveyance to the ice wells, while sheet ice was also harvested from the canal in the cold winters of those days, notwithstanding pollution from the gas works immediately upstream. From 1904, ice made in freezing plants largely supplanted natural ice here and

One of the ice wells under the London Canal Museum

the building was remodelled as a depot for the horses and carts that distributed the ice to customers, continuing as such until 1926.

The ubiquitous public works contractors John Mowlem & Co. had a stone wharf at Albert Wharf on the north-east corner of the basin in the late-19th and early-20th centuries, in succession to Messrs. Pratt and Sewell. There was an attractive curved boundary wall made out of old paving slabs and kerb stones, laid as rubble walling, but when the site was redeveloped in 1995-7 for expensive flats (Ice Wharf) this was trashed and replaced by a pathetic essay in crazy paving.

The Canalside Wharves east of the Basin

In the canal's early years a couple of coal merchants occupied wharves on the south side, opposite the towpath, to the east of Battlebridge Basin. All Saints Street was named after a plain brick church in mixed Gothic style, built 1837-8 next to Caledonian Road. It was demolished in 1975 after a fire.[21] Towards the street's west end at St James's Wharf, behind a smart-looking terrace of houses, the Ordnance Survey in 1871 showed three "lime kilns", where Coles Shadbolt and Co. had been making Roman Cement since 1852.[22] They also had a depot at the east end of the street at Thornhill Wharf, later numbered 123 Caledonian Road. A wharf cottage bearing their name in cement stucco remained until c.1990. Shadbolt's established a Portland Cement works at Harefield, Middlesex in 1880, sending the product to Caledonian Road by water.[23] They were succeeded after World War One by the Cement Marketing Co. and its corrugated-roofed cement store was still in use by a builders' merchant in 1975.

Coles Shadbolt, cement makers. All Saints Street, 1989

The Great Northern Railway's Granary, already noted, was the stimulus for Thomas Robinson to set up as a corn merchant at Pembroke Wharf in the 1850s, on the site of another Roman Cement wharf.[24] The canal was widened to provide a lay-by for barges. The 3-storey corn stores were arranged on two sides of a yard, with stables throughout the ground floor.[25] They were still there in 1952,[26] but later Bartlett's the export packers took over the premises and covered in the yard. The site was demolished for redevelopment c.1989-90 but the eastern range was re-erected as facsimile facades for an office building.

Lastly, Joseph Thorley and Sons were also in the milling business, but making cattle feed using ingredients such as oilseed that were mostly imported through the docks. Thorley moved from Hull to 4-6 All Saints Street (Victoria Wharf) around 1865, building a mainly 3-storey works surrounding a narrow yard.[27] This was mostly rebuilt to 4 storeys circa 1891, with an impressive red-brick and stone office frontage.[28] A substantial warehouse of 4½ storeys was built alongside the canal and later extended westwards at 5 storeys. The eastern part had massive wall-tie plates and no windows on the first, second and third floors facing the canal, before the office conversion of 1990-1, implying bins for bulk storage, although the loading doors served all levels. The western part had windows only in alternate bays. The firm was taken over by J Bibby and Sons in 1952 and put into voluntary liquidation in 1957.[29]

The Growth of Industry around the Basin

A new scale of development came to Battlebridge Basin in 1890-2 when the Westinghouse Brake Company, a prominent firm of railway engineers,

Thorley's former cattle feed mill, 1973

built a new head office and works at Middlesex Wharf, 82-86 York Road.[30] Their imposing office range in free-renaissance style by James Weir, FRIBA, of Victoria Street fronted York Way and the works extended back to the water's edge with a large chimney. From 1893, a foundry range with saw-tooth roofline was added and then extended to the north on part of Belmont Wharf.[31] After 1900, the rest of Belmont Wharf (90-94 York Road) was developed and a second office block was built, with a corner turret overlooking the canal. The architects were now Weir, Burrows and Weir.[32] The Belmont public house remained as an enclave until 1954.[33] Manufacturing moved to Chippenham in 1932 (it became the Westinghouse Brake and Signal Co. Ltd. in 1935), but the offices remained and they were extended across the north side of Belmont Wharf in 1956, in place of war-damaged workshops.[34] The offices closed in 1973 and the site was cleared in 1980.

Another firm of significant size was William J Plaistowe & Co, 'wholesale confectioners'. Plaistowe appeared in the street directories at Imperial Wharf and 40 Wharfdale Road from the mid 1870s. By 1910 the company had expanded to occupy Nos. 38, 40, 40A, 42 and 44B, and their extensive, 3-4 storey brick 'Jam, Preserve and Confectionery Factory' is shown on a Goad insurance plan of 1921.[35] The plan also shows them occupying two open wharves in New Wharf Road, partly with 'crates and empties', while these wharves are seen to be crowded with barrels for imported fruit in an Aerofilms photo of the same year.[36] There was further storage in other blocks. Within a few years there were new occupiers, the paper makers John Dickinson & Co. who rebuilt and extended the

Left: Canal looking W past Battlebridge Basin, 8 July 1973.

Right: Albert Wharf from NW with wall built of old paving stones, 28 July 1973.

Left: Entrance to Battlebridge Basin with Westinghouse works, 8 July 1973.

Right: Canal looking E from Maiden Lane Bridge, with tunnel in far distance, 28 July 1973.

Battlebridge Basin south end from E, with Porter's bottling works and Dickinson's former loading canopy, 15 March 1985

Westinghouse offices on Belmont Wharf (90-96 York Way)
from W, 3 May 1975

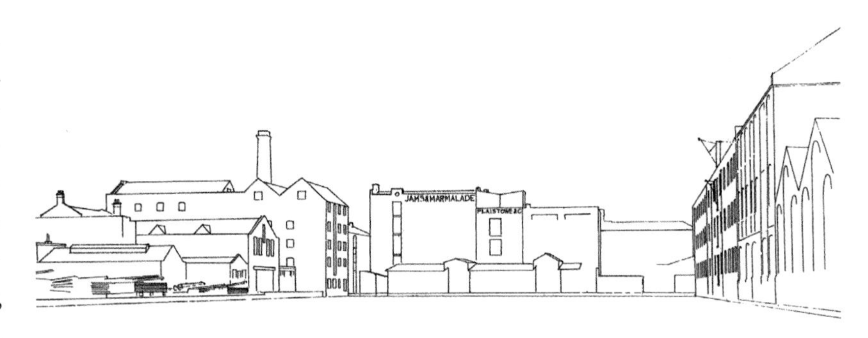

Battlebridge Basin from the north, 1969. From left to right: Timber yard in use, former Gatti ice depot, former flour mill, former salt warehouse, former Plaistowe's jam factory, Porter's bottling works, the Westinghouse Brake and Signal Co. *(Drawn by Malcolm Tucker from his photograph)*

premises as a stationery factory and brought paper by water from their mills in Hertfordshire.[37] It was unloaded under a steel and corrugated-sheet canopy. However, the basin elevation remained emblazoned 'Jams and Marmalade' until demolition in the late 1980s.

A third large firm was Robert Porter and Co. Ltd., on the west side of the basin at 4-14 Crinan Street. Like Plaistowe's, they depended on materials imported through the docks, in this case Guinness beer transported in barrels from Dublin, which they put into bottles and sent off by road. The taking-in doors and wall cranes can be seen on the basin side. They moved here in 1903, the date on the nice baroque-styled doorway near the northern end, and remained until around 1980. The street facade is embellished with smart red and blue engineering brickwork.

Between Crinan Street and York Way is the former British Legion Poppy Warehouse, where the poppies made by disabled servicemen in another part of London were stored ready for Remembrance Day. Presumably it was situated here because of the excellent rail services from the King's Cross Goods Station nearby. At 7 storeys plus a tank room, it was significantly the tallest building in the area when erected in the 1930s, and the eastern elevation sets back in a series of steps to reduce overshadowing. As a building exceeding the 250,000 cubic foot limit of the 1930 London Building Act, it required special scrutiny by the London County Council as to its safety against fire, but their case file appears not to survive. It would seem the major part of the building, at 70-76 York Road (York Way), was approved in 1932 and erected shortly afterwards, although it is uncertain if any of the 3-storey office on the main frontage is of that period.[38] The

The Poppy Warehouse and Mann Egerton's garage, from the south west, 1989

architects were Douglas and JD Wood of London W1. The rear elevation incorporates some older fabric. An extension northwards upon the site of 80 York Way was applied for in 1954 by the architects BW Turnbull and Partners of London EC4, with the tower lengthened and the offices built or extended to the street corner. Their architecture with soldier-course brickwork has a late-1930s feel.[39]

Another new building was a compact, 5-storey factory at the NE corner of the basin on part of Albert Wharf, built, it seems in the 1930s, as an extension of Thorley's cattle-food mill.[40] Charles Bartlett, export packers, later took over this and other premises along All Saints Street. Lastly, a 4-storey printing factory was built on the east side of New Wharf Road at No.20 (Swan House) around 1948. It was in the new post-war spirit, with

Eastern side of the basin in 1975, with disused timber yard on left

rendered concrete spandrels and long lines of flush glazing, but altered out of all recognition in an early 2000s conversion to publishers' offices.

Around 1890, the streets surrounding the basin had contained many businesses to do with horse transport – farriers, wheelwrights, a harness maker, a coach smith, a hay salesman, a bus company's offices. In the new century, connections with the motor industry developed, such as the London offices of the lorry builders Lacre at 78 York Way from c. 1910 to the mid 1930s. The bus manufacturers AEC used 12-13 New Wharf Road as a spare parts depot from the 1930s until the 1950s. After WW2, the high-class motor dealers Mann Egerton established a servicing centre at 68 York Way – their formerly smart garage building is now in another commercial use.

Decline and Redevelopment

When this writer first visited the area in the early 1970s it was in rapid decline from economic changes, although most premises were still occupied. Most noticeable then was the vacant timber yard at 15-16 New Wharf Road, although this later provided a haven for narrow-boat enthusiasts to moor. The site had been acquired circa 1970 by a consortium of architects and an engineering firm with the intention of building offices for their joint needs, and planning permission was granted on appeal in 1975.[41] A manhole was built to demonstrate the start of construction within the 5-year term of the permission, but economic conditions were not right. Later the site was able to be sold to a neighbouring property developer who was assembling land. The water of the Basin was owned until the 1980s by the surrounding owners jointly, as the Battlebridge Basin Company.[42]

In the 1980s the Greater London Council was also striving to purchase control of the Basin for socially sympathetic development, which in due course it did. The sites of Plaistowe's former jam factory and Haggis's timber yard were sold on to the Kingdomwide Housing Association, who built 4-storey houses and flats.[43] Porter's recently vacated bottling works was adapted for workshop units, completed in 1986.[44] However, the GLC was abolished by Margaret Thatcher's government with effect from April 1986 and its holdings had to be sold off. Porter's was then upgraded to offices, its northern half by the architects DEGW for their own use and the remainder by Fitch and Co.[45] The basin and sites on its east side were purchased in due course for private development by London Buildings PLC.

The water of the basin had become silted and rubbish-strewn by the 1970s. When the canal was drained down, two sunken cars were exposed. A turning point came in 1978 when the London Narrow Boat Association established moorings for its members at Albert Wharf. In 1984, with a grant from the GLC, they had the basin dredged.[46]

The Canal Museum Trust, through the perseverance of its then chairman, Dinah Hutchinson, acquired a lease of the demolished flour mill site from the dying GLC. It swapped it for a lease on the locally-listed ice wells site, which was less suitable for development and so came with a dowry, and then it was able to acquire the freehold at the bottom of the market in 1992, having opened the London Canal Museum to the public in April that

Old and new on the east side of the basin, November 2011

year. Various grants that were available helped with that. With some pain initially, the Museum has advanced successfully from there.

In the boom years of 1988-9, London Buildings promoted an 'air rights' development, for 3 storeys of offices on a bridge spanning the mouth of basin.[47] With giant tied arches of steel, it would have resembled on a smaller scale the building that spans the tracks out of Liverpool Street Station. The architects were David Marks and Julia Barfield. Controversially, it was given planning permission, but the scheme died in the following property slump, as did their associated proposals for office development along New Wharf Road.

Initiatives by other developers along All Saints Street were successful at that time. A partnership of the GLC's successor Greater London Enterprise with another developer produced an agreeable blend of new and retained fabric in the office development around courtyards on the Thorley's and

Robinson's sites, called Regent's Wharf and completed in 1991.[48] The architect was Rock Townsend. Less appealing is the sham warehouse office block at 123 Caledonian Road next door. The Peabody Trust's social housing scheme on the south side of All Saints Street had to wait till 1995 for approval.[49]

With reversals in the commercial market, London Buildings' strategy for the east side of the basin switched to residential. Between 1993 and 2000 they achieved an interesting mix of converted Industrial buildings and new build. Ashton's former salt warehouse and a manufacturing chemist's factory were divided into flats, called 'Gatti's Wharf', as was the Albert Wharf 5-storey factory, renamed 'Albert Dock', The new flats at 10 and 14 New Wharf Road and the 94-flat 'Ice Wharf' complex adopted distinctive bow-ended forms, by Munkenbeck and Marshall at No.10 (the site of the tall flour mill) and at No.14 and by Tchaik Chassay at 'Ice Wharf'. It is a pity that marketing people are so cavalier with historical names and terms such as Gatti, Ice and Dock, plucking them from their proper places and scattering them whimsically.

In 1992, the London Narrow Boat Association moved to new moorings at the south end of the basin, where they have a long lease. A walkway created around the south and east sides of the basin has remained gated, for the necessary reason of security. London Buildings established private moorings on the northern half, opened in 1999 and less greedy of water space than was initially proposed.[50] Their land-based developments being complete, London Buildings sold the basin's water area and the moorings to the navigation authority, British Waterways, in the year 2000 and departed from the scene.

To the west of the basin, beyond Crinan Street, the Poppy Warehouse at 70-78 York Way was converted in 1995-6 to residential 'lofts', with a luxury penthouse on top, and marketed as 'York Central'.[51] One large plot currently remains undeveloped there, at 62-68 York Way which also fronts Wharfdale Road and Crinan Street. Consent was granted on appeal in October 2008 for a mainly office scheme of 6 storeys plus a rooftop plant room, reducing to 4 storeys around the perimeter, although its philistine design by Tim Foster Associates had previously been rejected by the planning committee on grounds of bulk, massing and scale in relation to the Conservation Area.[52] The latest recession has held this back for the present.

It remains to discuss the Kings Place development, 90 York Way, on the site of the Westinghouse Brake and Signal Company at the north-west corner of the basin. Following site clearance in 1980, a range of low-rise warehouses was built there, clad in bright red brick but architecturally modest.[53] The southernmost bay incorporated a pub, the Waterside Inn, leased to Whitbread's, and the remains of a half-timbered barn were cut up to enliven this unprepossessing space.

With the warehouses being relatively new (and the pub a welcome place of refreshment in an area then somewhat lacking in such facilities), the proposals for Kings Place came as a surprise, as did the scale of the development – of 8 storeys and much bulkier than the Poppy Warehouse, in an area where 2 to 4 had been the norm. We have now grown used to that, thanks partly to the double-storeys device that breaks up the elevation facing the basin.

The planning application was submitted in October 2003 and finally approved in November 2004.[54] The architects were Dixon-Jones, i.e. Jeremy Dixon and Edward Jones and their colleagues. Construction commenced in 2005 with the deep basement excavation, strongly strutted across the corners, so the three tall, slip-formed concrete cores took quite some time to rise from the ground. When they were nearing completion, a fire involving gas cylinders at the top of the building closed the mainline railway for a day, for fear they would explode. Then the steelwork and other items started to arrive by water – one thinks that the clay from the excavations should also have travelled that way. Since completion in 2008, the presence of the concert halls, art galleries and restaurants and The Guardian newspaper as the principal tenant have certainly uplifted the area.

Malcolm Tucker is a Trustee of the London Canal Museum.

[1] Alan H Faulkner, *The Grand Junction Canal*, new edition, Rickmansworth, WH Walker Bros, 1993.

[2] 52 Geo3 cap. cxcv; Herbert Spencer, *London's Canal, An Illustrated History of the Regent's Canal,* second edition, London, Lund Humphries, 1976; Alan H Faulkner, *The Regent's Canal, London's Hidden Waterway*, Burton-on-Trent, Waterways World, 2005; Robert Philpotts, *When London Became an Island, The story of the building of the Regent's Canal,* London, Blackwater Books, 2008.

[3] Length as measured at 1 metre above the water line: information from Ken Baker, British Waterways tunnelling engineer at Leeds, 25 Feb 2002.

[4] Unlike the neighbouring owners the Thornhill family, little is known about William Horsfall, but as noted in Chapter 4 he owned most of Battle Bridge in the early 19th century. See Richard Dent's survey of Islington, 1805-6, Islington Local History Library.

[5] 59 Geo 3 cap. lxvi, clause 22.

[6] *Ibid.*

[7] Information from Ove Arup and Partners, consulting engineers.

[8] Faulkner, *op. cit.* (note 2), pp.28-9.

[9] *Ibid.*, p.29.

[10] *Ibid.*, p. 56.

[11] The writer is grateful to Alan Faulkner for his detailed notes on these matters taken from the Regent's Canal committee minutes in The National Archives, RAIL 860/8 onwards.

[12] George Cruikshank, 'London Going Out of Town or The March of Bricks and Mortar', 1829. See http://pressandpolicy.bl.uk/Resource-Library/View-Details-34f.aspx accessed 2012-03-23.

[13] One dust heap of mountainous proportion stood until 1826 at the corner of Gray's Inn Road, opposite where the 'Lighthouse' now is. For an illustration from the London Metropolitan Archives, see Gavin Stamp, 'From Battle Bridge to King's Cross: Urban Fabric and Change', in M Hunter and R Thorne (eds.), *Change at King's Cross*, London, Historical Publications, 1990, p.15.

[14] The tile kilns made roofing tiles, chimney pots, flower pots and drain pipes. They were more permanent structures than the improvised clamps and open-topped Scotch kilns of the brickfields, but nevertheless their locations moved northwards with time. They were at some distance from the Regent Quarter and Battlebridge Basin sites. The gas works continued in production until 1904-7.

[15] Ordnance Survey 1871; street directories; Victoria County History, Middlesex, Volume 8, Islington, pp.73-4.

[16] Robson's Directory for 1843, under 'Regent's Canal Wharfs'.

[17] London Metropolitan Archives, MR/UP/232, London & York Railway Bill, Deposited Plans, Nov. 1844, Part No.1, Map No.1.

[18] Street directories; Ordnance Survey maps at 5 feet to 1 mile surveyed 1871.

[19] Charles E Goad, Insurance Plan, London, Vol. XII, Sheet 399, March 1891.

[20] *Ibid.*

[21] Victoria County History, Middlesex, Volume 8, Islington, 1985, pp.88-99.

[22] Kelly's Post Office London Directory, 1852 onwards.

[23] AJ Francis, *The Cement Industry 1796-1914: A History,* Newton Abbot, David & Charles, 1977, p,174.

[24] Kelly's Post Office London Directory and Islington Directory, 1850s.

[25] Charles E Goad, Insurance Plan, London, Vol. XII, Sheet 399, March 1891

[26] Ordnance Survey 1:1250 plan, TQ 3083 SE, surveyed August 1952

[27] Street directories; Ordnance Survey, 1871. An article 'Thorley & Company, Cattle Food Manufacturers', in *Modern London: The World's Metropolis*, London, Historical Publishing Co., 1887, pp. 186-7, depicts a grandiose works only tenuously related to the site.

[28] Charles E Goad, Insurance Plan, London, Vol. XII, Sheet 399, March 1891, noting it was then under construction. A mill at the centre had '6 pair stones'.

[29] Harold W. Brace, *History of Seed Crushing in Great Britain*, London, 1960.

[30] London Metropolitan Archives, GLC/AR/BR/06/029410, block plan date-stamped 11 Aug 1890 (within a later building case file for the site).

[31] *Ibid.*, block plan date-stamped 24 May 1893.

[32] *Ibid.*, block plan date-stamped 28 Sept 1906, although that was to show a small alteration.

[33] Max Hoather (former employee) to Malcolm Tucker, personal communication and notes, 1993.

[34] *Ibid.*

[35] Charles E Goad, Insurance Plan, London, Vol. XII, Sheet 399, updated by overpasting to 1921, Camden Local Studies Centre.

[36] Copy held by the London Canal Museum.

[37] Grand Union Canal Company, *Arteries of Commerce*, London, n.d. (c.1935), p.23, under 'Horsfall Basin'.

[38] Kelly's Post Office London Directory, 1933 onwards; Ordnance Survey 1:1250 plan, TQ 3083 SW, surveyed August 1952; London Metropolitan Archives, GLC/AR/BR/13/102309, '80 York Way, British Legion Poppy Warehouse 1936-61'. The surviving building case file is for the post-war extension but it contains a letter of 29

July 1936 consenting 'a further deviation from the plans approved 12 December 1932 for reconstruction of the building at 70-76 York Road next to Crinan Street, to exceed 250,000 cubic feet, ...'

[39] *Ibid.*, but a basement plan is the only architect's drawing.

[40] C. E. Goad, Insurance Plan, London Vol XII, Sheet 399, updated by overpasting to 1939, London Metropolitan Archives

[41] Roger Rigby, 'Battlebridge Basin', Ove Arup Partnership Newsletter, No. 136, May 1983, pp.1-2.

[42] *Ibid.*; conversation between Malcolm Tucker and PJ Furnell, Managing Director of Robert Porter and Co. Ltd. and Trustee of the Battlebridge Basin Company, July 1977.

[43] LB Islington, planning application 862043, approved14 April 1987, architects Levitt Bernstein Associates.

[44] London Metropolitan Archives, GLC/DG/PRB/05/246, unveiling of plaque by Margaret Hodge, 1986. J Stewart had replaced Haggis in the timber yard's later years.

[45] Porter's North, LB Islington planning application 880774 approved 23 Feb 1989; Porter's South 880756 approved 9 Aug 1991.

[46] http://www.battlebridgemoorings.co.uk/history.htm accessed 2012-03-25; conversation with Fiona MacLean of the London Narrow Boat Association.

[47] LB Islington planning application 881021 of June 1988, approved 22 March 1989.

[48] LB Islington, planning applications 881290 and 900648; http://www.gle.co.uk/our-history.php and http://www.regenerate.co.uk/gle.htm accessed 2012-03-25.

[49] LB Islington planning application 931304 approved 24 march 1995, by Avanti Architects.

[50] LB Islington planning application 940063 of April 1994, approved with conditions 13 March 1997.

[51] LB Islington, planning application 940886, approved 16 Aug 1995.

[52] LB Islington, planning application P070753, refused at committee on 08 Nov 2007 but allowed on appeal. The consent was renewed via a new application P110506 on 30 June 2011. Other bulky schemes had been approved in the 1990s but not implemented.

[53] Consented 7 May 1980, architects Elsom Pack & Roberts. The developers were P&O Properties, as it happens, but that was unrelated to the Regent Quarter, two blocks southward.

[54] LB Islington, planning application P032145 for 82-96 York Way, London N1, name later changed to 90 York Way.

Chapter 6

Kings Place

Introduction

Kings Place, an innovative arts and business centre, is situated to the north of the campaign areas previously described. It sits well with new buildings in the Regent Quarter and in Battlebridge Basin.

Peter Millican, owner and entrepreneur, was inspired when he chose to build it by the side of the Regent's Canal. As soon as one descends from the noisy York Way to the ground floor on tow path level there is a sense of unwinding one's snarls, of being alive and yet peaceful, of being stimulated and yet calm.

It has been open since October 2008 from early morning to late at night. Here the public, local schools and communities can enjoy the visual arts, all kinds of music, poetry and comedy or simply eat a snack or dine. There are many places to sit, including the terrace by the canal outside the Rotunda Restaurant, or inside the building along the generously large table under the atrium, or in the comfortable leather chairs spread out in the foyer. It is a good place to relax, to meet friends or to talk business.

It is hoped that the following pages give a fuller view of this very active and stimulating space.

Angela Inglis

Kings Place – the architect's story

by Sir Jeremy Dixon, *architect of Kings Place*

Working on the new building at Kings Place has been a privilege. It is unusual for an architect to work with a client with such a clear and radical vision. Now functioning as planned, the building complex has an extraordinary range of arts and social facilities supported by a commercial office development. It was Peter Millican's main vision that the building should be open to the public and make a substantial contribution to the cultural life of the city.

Most office developments are closed to the public and, as a result, give little back to the street life of the surrounding city. This would be typical of almost all buildings in the city of London. It is in this context that Peter's project can be seen to be so radical, every part of the design process reflects his thinking. Indeed, one can see the whole enterprise as a representation of Peter's personal interests and tastes (he loves all kinds of music, the visual arts, sculpture, a good meal, etc) and this is a strength not a weakness. I believe that it is part of the special nature of the Kings Place proposition that it derives from the client's personal interests – the building extends his own world. It is this committed position that provides the strength behind the provision of the cultural spaces for the public.

Music takes the form of two concert halls and a generous arrangement of rehearsal and studio spaces which become the home of two major London orchestras; the London Sinfonietta, and the Orchestra of the Age of Enlightenment. Typical of Peter, we were all taken to Tokyo to look at small concert halls, for some reason there are more examples in Japan than in Europe. This was a formative trip giving us thoughts about the treatment of the 'shoe box' type of interior. The good acoustics are the result of many detailed considerations under the guidance of the acoustician Rob Harris. The proportions and volume matter, but the real challenge is to provide articulated detail to the interior surfaces of the hall that distribute sound and prevent reverberance. Here we introduced the columns, the coffered ceiling, and the multitude of random patterns sculpted into the timber.

One memorable trip was followed by another, this time to choose the timber to make the veneer linings of the halls. We were taken to darkest Germany where giant oak trees grow amongst beeches, driving them tall and straight towards the sky. These special trees have their own names and the one that we ended up with was called 'Contessa'. We were shown round the timber yard and how the veneer was cut with giant sliding knives. Afterwards, in discussion, the owners said that they had a very special tree that they didn't want divided up – this was Contessa. As it turned out, this single tree provided all the linings to both halls and the seats. Entering for a concert at Kings Place one can imagine oneself to be in the middle of a single giant oak tree.

The second hall is square in plan and was intended to be firstly a rehearsal space for the orchestras. In fact it has become a successful multi-use performance space complimenting the more structured nature of Hall 1. Generous foyers connect the open ground floor to the two basement levels. Access to the halls is via an escalator. It was by digging a huge hole in the ground and using new techniques for retaining the earth, that such generosity of space was made possible. There was a dramatic moment when the 80m square 15m deep hole sat, empty, with the water in the canal hovering precariously on two sides.

Again, we have to thank Peter for the choice of the site. Close to Kings Cross and St Pancras, it has the very special advantage of being able to relate both internal and external spaces to water. It is extraordinary how much the whole environment changes as one descends from the noise of York Way down to the quiet of the tow path. The Rotunda restaurant sits on the corner between two stretches of water. It is a high class restaurant run by Peter in partnership with John Nugent. The circular layout emphasises the views and limits the scale of the interior. With its special granite bar surface, dark woods, and blue leather, the restaurant is intended to reflect the general style of the overall building. The rest of the ground floor is open to the public with informal eating and a super-long table for everyone to sit round. There are places with comfortable chairs and a general sense of welcome to anyone who chooses to come into the building. Whether

King's Place canal side terrace.
Photo: Angela Inglis

it is sharing the arts facilities with local schools and communities, or introducing broadly based programming in the halls, Peter has always emphasised inclusiveness and accessibility.

The commercial offices occupy the seven floors above ground, they are conventional open plan, and have been taken by the Guardian and Observer amongst others. The local planning authority, Islington, was worried about the scale of the building. This was before the Argent scheme opposite had begun its own much larger building programme. To respond to these concerns, Kings Place has two contrasting faces. Towards the canal, the building breaks up into several separated pure forms linked by bridges. Along York Way the façade is all glass but of a very particular nature. Sustainability has meant that this façade has three layers of glass, the outer one being free of the structure of the building. This enables it to take on its own geometry which is based on extremely shallow curves in glass. These curves only make sense when seen looking up and down York Way, the main approach to the building. Here they coalesce into stronger sculpted curves that look like the rippling of water. Sustainability has been a key aspect of the project, Peter having expressed clear ambitions in this area well before the more fashionable movement presently influencing architectural projects.

With its orchestras, galleries, restaurants, outreach to the local communities, and the diverse programming of its halls, Kings Place is a new kind of building type for London, suggesting that developers and their buildings can be more adventurous and positive in the contributions they make to the cultural and urban life of the city.

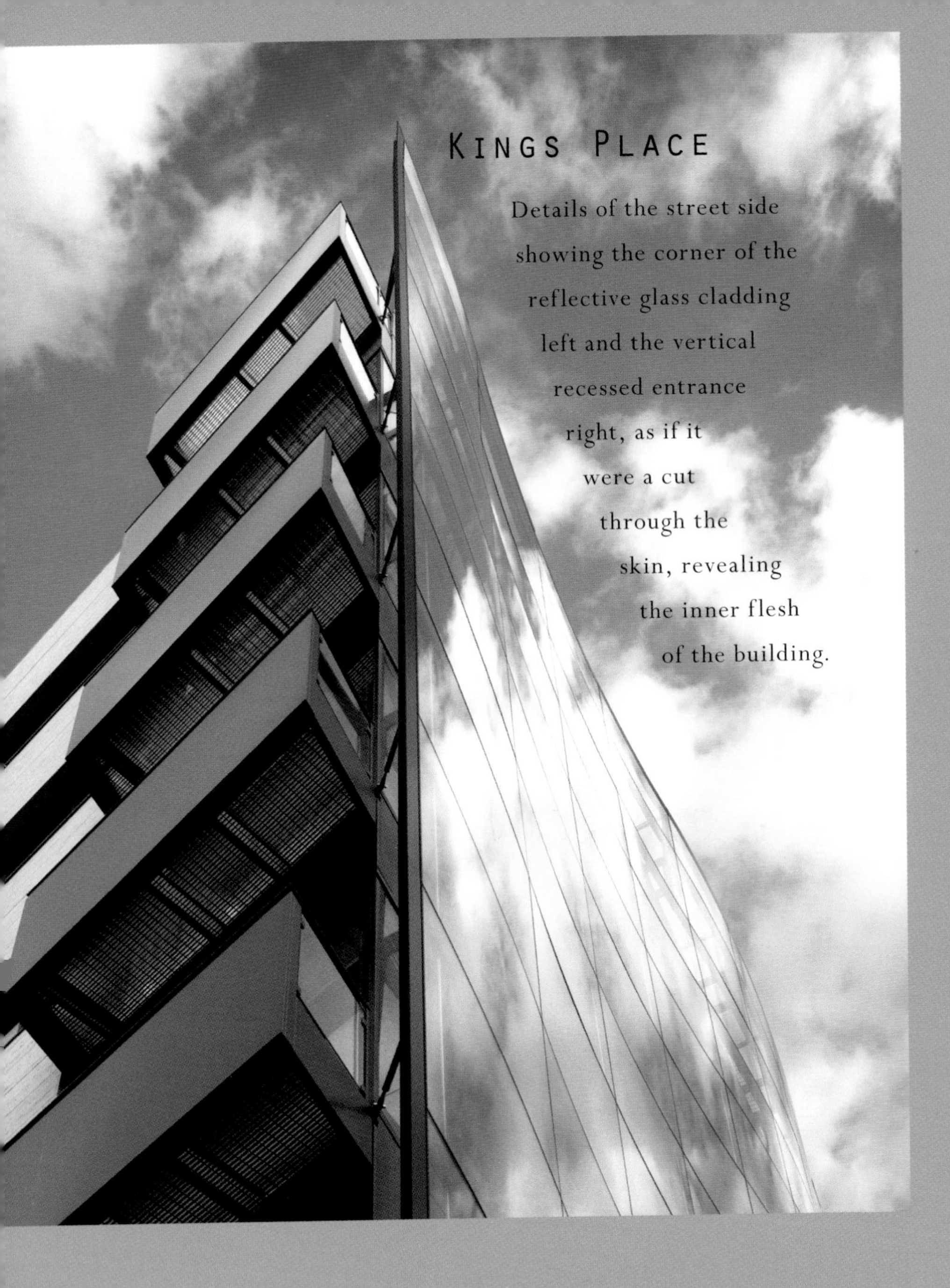

Kings Place

Details of the street side showing the corner of the reflective glass cladding left and the vertical recessed entrance right, as if it were a cut through the skin, revealing the inner flesh of the building.

kings place

Kings Place

Left: Looking south with the undulating glass cladding facing York Way and side of building adjoining the Regent's Canal.
Right: Corner detail of glass cladding at the canal end.

Kings Place

Left: The street side of Kings Place. Showing the gentle undulation and corner detail of the reflective glass cladding.
Below: The entrance to the Guardian and Observer newspaper offices at the corner of York Way and Crinan Street.

Kings Place

Looking up from the main floor, showing how the building's geometry continues to the inner roof.

Kings Place - the conservation angle

by Alec Forshaw

This wonderful scheme could never have happened if the Marks Barfield scheme for an office bridge across Battle Bridge Basin had gone ahead. One side of the bridge would have occupied the Westinghouse site. Ice Wharf wouldn't have happened either on the other side.

When Peter Millican first came in to see us at the Islington Planning Department he said that he was looking at various sites in London. I could tell immediately that he had an exceptional vision, totally different from the normal developer, and that we should do all we could to get him to commit to Islington.

We explained what was going on in the King's Cross area, including our long-standing grant scheme, the P&O proposals, and we also shared our enthusiasm for his vision for creating a major new arts venue. I told him about the St Luke's LSO project which was well under way at the time.

There were quite a lot of objections to the original submitted proposals of Dixon Jones, particularly the bulk of the offices, their height and the apparent blandness of the façade to York Way. Jeremy Dixon and I worked, I think, very well together on this, and I visited their offices (at that time in Chalk Farm) several times as the scheme evolved. They came up with the 'wavy' frontage, and I suggested breaking it in two, with a recess marking the main entrance. On Battlebridge Basin we modified the bulk to reduce its impact. In retrospect, while it has perhaps established a greater scale on the Islington side of York Way than had existed before, it is nothing to what is proposed on the Camden side!

In terms of the quality of materials and quality of finish this is one of the very best new buildings in Islington. The generosity and vision of the developer, and the assiduous attention to detail by Dixon Jones, was magnificent. It's as good a building as the Royal Opera House. The popularity of the public areas is surely evidence that quality pays. It deservedly won the Islington Society Design Award in 2008. The Regent Quarter had won the same award in 2006.

As someone with a strong interest in the performing arts, Kings Place together with St Luke's Old Street is one of the two individual building projects with which I am most pleased to have been involved during my 32 years at Islington. How could I have dreamt in 1988 that two new major concert halls would be created in Islington over the next twenty years?

Battlebridge Basin
Photo: Angela Inglis

Kings Place

The external structure at the rear on the canal side continues within the internal structure of Kings Place. The image on the right shows the exit at the rear of the building. This is opposite the entrance on the street side, enabling easy access from one environment to the other.

KINGS PLACE

Two views of a similar perspective showing the construction and finished building. The beginnings of the rotunda can be seen in the image on the left, clustered around the central tower.

Kings Place barge transport by Gerard Heward

Loading cladding panels into a Dutch Barge
Photo: Gerard Heward

Scouser, Dutch Barge arriving at Kings Place.
Photo: Gerard Heward

In September 2006 Wood, Hall & Heward Ltd were contacted by Sir Robert McAlpine with regards to the possibility of delivering construction materials to a canal side site in the King's Cross area – Kings Place.

McAlpine were prompted to investigate alternative options as a result of a combination of local objections to lorry deliveries to the site on the busy York Way and very limited storage space for the materials. As the site has the canal on two sides, canal transport was the obvious choice.

It was decided that Wharf Road was a better place for all the construction materials to be delivered to, since at that time, McAlpine's site offices were located here in the railway sidings, across the road from the Kings Place development. McAlpine built a pedestrian shelter over the towpath and installed a temporary crane on Wharf Road adjacent to the canal, creating a loading bay for materials to be loaded into the canal barges below.

A Bantam Pusher Tug was used to transport the 60 tonne barges, loaded with steel beams and other materials from the Wharf Road loading bay to the Kings Place development site. Once at the site the two canal side tower cranes would unload the barges ready for the next load.

Other contractors who followed, encouraged by the success McAlpine's had with the delivery of steel beams for the steel frame erection stage, continued to use the barges for the delivery of their construction materials. These materials included granite faced cladding panels, stair cases, windows and the exterior glazing system.

At its peak 5 barges were on site at any time effectively creating an additional 50m by 8m area of storage alongside the site. The convenience of having building materials sitting in a barge alongside the site increased the efficiency of the tower cranes as items could be picked up and used as and when needed rather than having to stack, store and move materials several times for them to be in the correct place.

In addition to the above, some construction waste was also removed from the site by barge including all the plaster board waste which went to Powerday's canal side recycling facility in Willesden.

Over a period of about 18 months hundreds of tonnes of building materials were delivered to the Kings Place site by barge.

Kings Place

View of the terrace outside the Rotunda restaurant.

Kings Place

View of Battlebridge basin from the terrace looking through a sculpture by Lynn Chadwick. This sculpture can also be seen on page 209.

Sculpture at Kings Place

Left: Looking up at the rotunda by Battlebridge Basin.
Ann Christopher, Dark Line, Bronze, Edition of 3.
Photo courtesy: Ann Christopher/ Pangolin London.
Right: Lynn Chadwick, Monitor, Bronze, Edition of 4.
Photo courtesy: Lynn Chadwick/ Pangolin London.

Sculpture at Kings Place

Sculptures located on the basin and canal side terrace.

Below: Terence Coventry, Monumental Steel Bull, Powdercoated steel, Unique.

Photo courtesy: Terence Coventry/Pangolin London.

Right: Jon Buck, Dove, Bronze, Edition of 9. *Photo courtesy: Jon Buck/Pangolin London.*

Kings Place

Photographer Chris Steele-Perkins signs a book from the "England, My England" exhibition at Kings Place Gallery, June 2010.

Kings Place

Previous Pangolin London Sculptor in Residence Abigail Fallis with Tuna Fish (with strings attached), Bronze with steel strings, Unique. Fallis in Wonderland exhibition.

Kings Place

There are two commercial galleries at Kings Place: Kings Place Gallery and Pangolin London.

Left: Kings Place Gallery, "Line of Influence: Portraits of Central Saint Martins" by Janet Lance-Hughes at Kings Place Gallery, Jan 2011

Right: Pangolin London. Abigail Fallis, Queen of Hearts, Steel, vinyl and resin, Edition of 3.

Photo courtesy: Abigail Fallis/ Pangolin London.

SACCONI QUARTET

Sacconi Quartet, Kings Place Festival, 2010.

Photo: Chris Tribble.

Sarod Players

Amaan Ali Khan and Ayaan Ali Khan, the virtuosi "sarod" players.

Kings Place Festival 2009. *Photo: Chris Tribble.*

Performance

Left: Mellow Baku, Kings Place Festival 2009. ***Right:*** Harry Winstanley, flute (Royal Academy of Music), Kings Place Festival 2010. *Photos: Chris Tribble.*

Kings Place - a user's view

by Lauren Shanley

I waited with great interest for the building to be ready, thrilled that there were to be more concert halls and exhibition spaces to visit. Another new place to add to the regeneration of King's Cross.

It opened with a great celebration and a host of free entertainment in all disciplines. I was there and loved it.

Since then I have been back many times and seen a huge range of exciting and unusual performances not available in other venues in London.

I love the main concert halls for the extensive range of classical music concerts, the Base for jazz, more experimental music and panel discussions, and the free performances in the foyer area.

Being an artist myself, and interested in a wide variety of art, I enjoy the exhibitions in the galleries and public spaces. These are full of height and light. They are a real joy as they are big enough to never feel over-crowded.

The building itself is a very useable space to relax in, have coffee, good food, meet friends, enjoy the ambience of sitting outside in amongst the sculptures by the canal, and if you go early enough you have it all to yourself.

A rare treat in the centre of London.

Kings Place - the locals' view

by Jim & Lana Humphris

Having lived in Camden Town for over 40 years we have enjoyed many of the cultural delights of the area as well as their extraordinary diversity and multi-ethnicity. Many of these venues are to the west and north of where we live; while to the south lies the railway lands of King's Cross and St Pancras, now undergoing a massive regeneration programme. One of the first significant developments here was Kings Place, a handsome landmark building overlooking Regent's Canal and less than twenty minutes walk from our house.

How convenient and what a gem! Consistently Kings Place has offered a wide variety of top quality cultural activities with classical, folk, jazz and contemporary music mixed with art exhibitions; all set in a modern, open and well thought out space. Last year's Mozart Unwrapped series provided not only something for everyone but also an extensive insight into Mozart's virtuosity. In 2012 we will be enjoying the complementary Brahms series along with comedy and spoken word events and a range of contemporary concerts. On-line saver tickets can be bought for £9.50 and that's a bargain!

Kings Place is not only a concert hall, it boasts a welcoming interior suitable as an anytime meeting place, a coffee morning with relatives, friends or business associates, a place for a quiet lunch by the canal or for fine dining at the Rotunda restaurant.

Kings Place is a fine example of an office block open to the public, a genuine multi-use building enhancing the cultural landscape. It's wonderful to see it being used by so many and so often; and it's only a short walk from home!

Phil Jeffries.
Photo: Diana Shelley

Tribute by Diana Shelley

Phil Jeffries, 1953–2008

Phil Jeffries was born in Darlington and came to London to study physiology. He dropped out and became involved in various radical campaigns in the 1970s, including the squatting movement where he acquired legal knowledge which helped save many people from homelessness. Later, he was active in the peace movement and co-edited a *Legal Advice Pack for Nuclear Disarmers*, published by CND in 1984.

From 1987 to his death, he was at the heart of the struggle to protect King's Cross and make a better place for the community there. He helped found the King's Cross Railway Lands Group, serving as chair in three separate years. With other activists, he saw off the original plan to bring the Channel Tunnel Rail Link underneath London to King's Cross, and in 1994 helped found Cally Rail Group to fight the negative impacts when the route switched to St Pancras.

His brilliant analytical skills, talent for lobbying and ability to work with almost anyone helped minimise the impacts of CTRL in West Islington. When in 2001, ignoring a Parliamentary decision, CTRL decided to dig up the Cally Road for 15 months, Phil led negotiations with the Department for Transport which won a special compensation scheme for shopkeepers whose trade was disrupted; £100,000 was successfully claimed. In 2003–4 he worked with residents in St Pancras to win an appeal against CTRL's attempt to extend noisy work around the clock. His final years were devoted to the unsuccessful campaign to get a better development at King's Cross Central.

Phil held various jobs until in 1985 he went to work for the Greater London Council. After abolition he worked for the Fire and Civil Defence Authority, then the London Fire Brigade, where he became its statistician.

A trade unionist, sceptical Labour Party member but always committed to social justice, Phil played some part in most of the campaigns in this book. He would have been proud to share its dedication with his comrade, Lisa Pontecorvo.

Lisa Pontecorvo depicted at the head of a march in a mural tribute to the Tolpuddle Martyrs.
Photo: Angela Inglis

Tribute by Andrew Bosi

Lisa Pontecorvo, 1944–2008

I was delighted to hear that this book is dedicated to Lisa Pontecorvo and Phil Jeffries, who between them did so much to retain the sense of place that King's Cross holds.

Lisa worked tirelessly both to prevent wanton demolition and for positive change. The new Regent Quarter, described in this book, would have been very different without her campaign to retain the heritage buildings that give King's Cross its sense not only of place but of time. More than a century and a half of history remains on our doorstep.

Between 2000 and 2007 Lisa ran the Cally shopfront competition with Alec Forshaw. These awards helped revive the Cally's appearance at a time when it seemed the benefits of "gentrification" had passed it by.

You will read of the wasteland that was King's Cross. Nowhere was this more true than in Edward Square, the pinnacle of Lisa's career. The squares of Islington are almost all not square, but most are fashionable. Edward Square was neither, and it took years of persistent campaigning to save it for community use. After funding had been secured to redesign it, the campaign helped revive community activity using the newlycreated open space. When Lisa died in 2008, the nearby Tolpuddle Martyrs' mural was repainted to include her, appropriately at the head of the procession.

Within walking distance of King's Cross, there are other reminders of Lisa's work for conservation: the Matilda Street chimney, the *Drapers Arms* public house, and the roof scape of Caledonian Road. It was Lisa's campaign to limit the proliferation of Mansard roofs that persuaded Islington council to adopt a more consistent policy towards roof extensions.

Lisa also rescued many local organisations' archives from destruction. Future historians of King's Cross can find these invaluable records in the London Metropolitan Archives.

Acknowledgements

This book has been a collaborative effort and could not have been produced without the help of many people. Any errors or omissions are of course my responsibility (Angela Inglis).

Thanks to those who contributed in writing: Mike Bruce, Andrew Bosi, Anthony Delarue, Sir Jeremy Dixon, Alec Forshaw, Gerard Heward, Jim and Lana Humphris, Rob Inglis, Randal Keynes, Martin Lipson, Paul Lowenberg, Peter Millican, Lester Pritchard, Lauren Shanley, Peter Shaw, Diana Shelley, Lord Chris Smith and Malcolm Tucker.

Thanks to those who contributed maps, plans, drawings, paintings and photographs: Gary Brooks, Camden Local Studies and Archives, Anthony Delarue, E C Harris, Gerard Heward, Chris Hollick, Islington Local History Centre, Randal Keynes, P&O, RHWL, Lord Chris Smith, Norma Steel and her family and friends, Chris Tribble (Kings Place), Malcolm Tucker.

Thanks to the following individuals and organisations for help with information and research: Kristie Bishop (Drink, Shop & Do), Mike Bruce, Gary Brooks, Camden Local Studies and Archives, Pat Clough, Aron Cronin, WCS Digital Print, Alec Forshaw, David Harter, Mary Henkel, Margaret Hodge MP, Housmans (Albert Beale), Islington Local History Centre (Mark Aston), Barbara Jacobson, King's Cross Conservation Area Advisory Committee, King's Cross Development Forum, King's Cross Railway Lands Group, King's Cross Voices Oral History Project (Leslie McCartney), Kings Place staff (Polly Bielecka, Alexandra Darby, Nicola Euden and Emrah Tokalac), Lucinda Lambton, Martin Lipson, Paul Lowenberg, Dennis Mannina, David McGillivray, Pauline Nee, Lester Pritchard, Val and Tony Rees, Lord Chris Smith, Norma Steel, Liz and Bob Stuckey and WCS Digital Print.

Special thanks to Tim Burnett for editing King's Cross: A Sense of Place, and for additional input from Cathy Aitchison; and very special thanks to Nigel Buckner for his design expertise.

The book could not have been produced without the help and support of Jeannie Burnett, Peter Millican, Diana Shelley and Norma Steel.